Hampton University: A National Treasure

Hampton University: A National Treasure
A Documentary History from 1978 to 1992

Dr. Martha E. Dawson

Venture Books
Beckham House Publishers, Inc.
Silver Spring, MD

Copyright 1994, Hampton University

All rights reserved. Printed in the U.S.A.

No part of this publication may be reproduced or transmitted in any form or by any means, electronic or mechanical, including photocopy, recording or any information storage and retrieval system now known or to be invented, without permission in writing from the publisher, except by a reviewer who wishes to quote brief passages in connection with a review written for inclusion in a magazine, newspaper or broadcast.

Published in the United States by
Beckham House Publishers, Inc.
P.O. Box 8008, Silver Spring, MD 20907

ISBN: 0-931761-36-0

10 9 8 7 6 5 4 3 2 1

TABLE OF CONTENTS

Acknowledgments..i

Contributors..iii

Introduction...vii

1   A Glorious Past: Leaders, Buildings, and Events..................1

2   The New President...9

3   The Inaugural Address of Dr. William R. Harvey................15

4   The President's Impact.......................................24

5   A New Academic Model..46

6   Fund Raising, 1978-1990......................................51

7   Faculty Leadership..59

8   A Period of Prosperity..76

9   Hampton is for Students......................................98

10 Academics: Heart of the University...........................119

11 Faculty, Staff, Students, and Alumni Accept
    the Challenge of Change....................................154

Epilogue..170

References..180

Index...182

ACKNOWLEDGMENTS

First and foremost, I would like to express gratitude to President William R. Harvey for granting me the sabbatical to engage in the writing of this book during my transitional year from vice president to professor emeritus. I have been especially fortunate to have the resources of Hampton University at my disposal while I have pursued this effort. The administrators and staff of The Hampton University Center for Teaching Excellence have been invaluable in assisting me: Jeanette Singleton, John Alewenyse and especially its director, Linda C. Petty.

I seriously doubt that I could have accomplished this task without the concern, advice and technical assistance of individuals in the center. Special thanks is given to Kathleen Duff, my secretary and research assistant, for her professional skills, patience, and assistance in collecting data. Her efforts have made this a more coherent publication. Above all, I give my deepest appreciation to colleagues at the university--some who are no longer with us--who responded to the data collection instruments, thereby providing primary information for this contemporary history.

It would have been impossible to compile this documentary profile of Hampton University without the written information submitted by vice presidents, deans, directors, chairs and coordinators. These individuals were the prime movers in developing the higher education model which evolved during the period of this study.

I am also grateful to those who shared their special talents with me as I attempted to bring ideas into focus: Kawabena Ampofo-Anti, associate professor of art, who took the disjointed ideas I had and developed the cover design; Adebisi Oladipupo, assistant professor of engineering, who turned raw data into meaningful graphic representations; and Ayuba J. Sarki, chair of the department of economics, who provided thoughtful comments on economic data.

It would have been impossible to write this book without the assistance of Fritz Malval, university archivist, and his staff. They provided notebook files of news clippings. Kathy Edwards and the staff in the office of university relations made the complete news release files available. I received a great deal of help from Jean Watts,

Wanola Rose and Sharon White of the Office of the President. These professionals took time from their busy schedules to accommodate innumerable requests made for reports and other documents. I deeply appreciate this assistance.

Special appreciation and recognition are given to Mr. Ruben Burrell, university photographer, whose creative genius continues to provide a remarkable graphic view of Hampton University.

I wish to pay special tribute to Dr. Joyce Jarrett who challenged my thoughts and gave me impossible deadlines as she painstakingly edited my writing. I am also grateful to Elnora Daniel, incumbent vice president for academic affairs, for her friendship and support as I plodded through the writing of this book.

This book is a result of enumerable professional opportunities and support given me by President William R. Harvey during my 12-year tenure as vice president of academic affairs as well as the continued professional involvement I now enjoy with the institution. And finally, I would like to thank Barry Beckham and his editorial staff at Beckham House for guiding me through the publication of this book.

Martha E. Dawson

CONTRIBUTORS

The writer sent a survey to those who had held positions of leadership at Hampton during 1978-1991. Data from the individuals below were used along with information from annual reports, departmental records, news briefings, printed media documents, special reports and interviews in the writing of this documentary history of Hampton University.

NAME	POSITION
Dr. John Alewynse	Professor of English Dean of Freshman Studies, 1990-91
Mr. Robert Askew	Instructor, Department of Accounting and Finance School of Business
Dr. Earl Bean	Director of Libraries and Satellite Center
Dr. David T. Beaty	Associate Professor, Department of Management School of Business
Dr. Robert D. Bonner	Dean, School of Pure and Applied Sciences
Dr. Carlton E. Brown	Dean, School of Liberal Arts and Education
Dr. Alphonse C. Carter	Dean, School of Business
Mr. Laron J. Clark, Jr.	Vice President for Development
Mr. LeCount Conaway	Director of Sports Information

Contributors

Dr. Harold W. Conley	Assistant Vice President for Academic Affairs
Mrs. Jorsene Cooper	Interim University Registrar
Dr. Elnora D. Daniel	Former Dean, School of Nursing Vice President for Academic Affairs (July 1991-)
Mrs. Vivian David	Director, Alumni Affairs
Mr. Rufus Easter	Director, Auxiliary Services
Mr. Frank B. Edgcombe	Periodicals Librarian
Dr. Larnell Flannagan	Chair, Department of Education School of Liberal Arts and Education
Dr. Hazel Garrison	Professor Emeritus of Biology and Former Dean of the Graduate College
Dr. Enid P. Housty	Director of the Humanities Program School of Liberal Arts and Education
Dr. Reginald Jones	Chair, Department of Psychology School of Liberal Arts and Education
Dr. William Kearney	Former Chair, Department of Mass Media Arts School of Liberal Arts and Education Former Dean, School of Arts and Letters Professor Emeritus, Mass Media Arts
Mr. Alphonso Knight	Former Director of Alumni Affairs Former President, National Hampton Alumni, Inc.

Dr. Willie O. Lawton	Dean, College of Continuing Education
Mrs. Barbara M. Lamb	Circulation Librarian
*Atty. Ray L. LeFlore	Former Chair, Board of Trustees
Ms. Marilyn N. Loesch	Reference Librarian
Mrs. Eleanor Lynch	Former Director, The Honors College Associate Director, Center for Teaching Excellence
Mr. Fritz J. Malval	University Archivist
Dr. Linda C. Petty	Director, Center for Teaching Excellence
Dr. Oscar Prater	Former Vice President for Administrative Services (1980-1990) President, Fort Valley State University
Dr. Edward Pyatt	Professor, Department of Accounting and Finance School of Business
Ms. Cora M. Reid	Library Clerk
Dr. Diane Q. Robinson	Director, Interdisciplinary Science Center
Dr. Ayuba J. Sarki	Chair, Department of Economics School of Business
Dr. Robert M. Screen	Chair, Department of Communication Disorders School of Pure and Applied Sciences

*Responded via telephone

Mrs. Joyce Taylor	Federal Relations Officer Office of Development
Dr. Isai T. Urasa	Chair, Department of Chemistry School of Pure and Applied Sciences
Major Claude Vann, III	Assistant Professor Department of Military Science
Dr. Demetrius D. Venable	Vice President for Research and Dean of the Graduate College
Dr. James Victor	Associate Director, National Center for Minority Special Education Research and Outreach
Dr. Harold E. Wade	Former Executive Vice President
Mrs. Peggy A. Wallace	Former Director, Assessment and Learning Support Center
Mr. John W. Watkins	Coordinator, Trio Program
Mrs. Julia G. Williams	Former Director, H. U. Laboratory School
Dr. Greer D. Wilson	Former Director of Student Activities and Student Union, Hampton University Director, Newcome Student Center, University of Virginia
Mr. Lucius C. Wyatt	Former Vice President for Fiscal Affairs and Treasurer
Dr. Hoda M. Zaki	Chair, Department of Political Science School of Liberal Arts and Education

INTRODUCTION

My aim is to present a contemporary history in documentary form of the small, multicultural, comprehensive university called Hampton University. I hope to provide some insight into the inner workings of one of the nation's premier institutions of higher education during the post-civil rights era of the twentieth century. Accordingly, the work focuses on the period from 1978--with the selection of current President William R. Harvey--to the 1992 academic year.

This is a personal documentary about the people and events that shaped the direction of a national treasure, a remarkable 124-year-old historically black university. In particular, my focus is on how Hampton University, under the guidance of a new chief administrator, made the transformation in the last 14 years from a small college to a comprehensive university.

I call it a personal documentary because I wanted to write a history that is more personalized than the typical work of scholarship, and I wanted to offer documentation in the form of actual texts, lists and charts that give a feel for the human touch of the institution.

A key component of Hampton's transformation is the university's moving from a predominantly teaching-oriented faculty to one that assumed a leadership position in research and grantsmanship. At the same time, the faculty maintained nevertheless its commitment to teaching and service to both students and their profession.

Hampton's story in the last quarter century, because of the challenges encountered, is in certain respects a microcosm of all small institutions of higher education--black or white. These were years when all collegiate institutions were faced with budget deficits, erratic patterns of growth, more diverse student populations and a gradual erosion of public confidence about the quality and value of American higher education.

Hampton University (formerly Hampton Normal and Agricultural Institute from 1868 to 1930; and Hampton Institute from 1930 to 1984) represents an educational cornerstone in America. From its very beginning it has presented exciting models for other institutions of higher education. Hampton opened its doors at the great transitional period in America's history: the shackles of slavery had been recently removed from black people and now the burden of segregation was placed on their shoulders. However, through the dreams, hard work, dedicated leadership and genius of both white and black citizens, Hampton prospered during this watershed period and developed into an outstanding college in both the eras of segregation and post-civil rights revolution. Even with the civil disorders which interrupted the progress of universities throughout America in the sixties, the administrative structure at Hampton survived and flourished.

Hampton has always championed a high regard for multicultural diversity. This strong commitment might well serve as a model for those in American higher education who now find it difficult to create a learning community in which faculty and students of different cultural, racial and socioeconomic backgrounds can live and learn together.

And since its founding, Hampton University continues to be a prototype of service. Its unique contribution to higher education in general and to the educational development of the African diaspora in particular has yet to be adequately documented. In fact, little, if any attention has been given to the success and contributions of a unique group of institutions of higher education that have come to be known in the last quarter of the twentieth century as "Historically Black Colleges and Universities (HBCU's)." While the impressive histories of such prestigious institutions as Yale, Harvard, The College of William and Mary, Stanford, Princeton, Oberlin, Massachusetts Institute of Technology, The University of Notre Dame, and The University of Virginia are noted with fanfare, there is too little celebration about the philosophies and inner workings of HBCU's.

Despite political and economic adversity, these institutions have made significant contributions to the growth and development of our nation by educating those whose ancestors were brought to these United States to be chained in the shackles of slavery, later restrained by segregation, and even in this last decade of the twentieth century to be restricted by racism, poverty and prejudice. Despite this oppression, the group that has been identified variously as nigger, colored, negro, Afro-American, black American and currently African American have, like their more privileged counterparts, contributed significantly to the rich heritage of the United States.

Many of the contributions made by these African Americans were made possible by the work of the thousands who labored to establish such institutions like Howard University in Washington, D.C., Spelman College and Morehouse College in Atlanta, and Fisk University in Nashville. The founders of those early HBCU's were compassionate and visionary white people, dedicated to providing opportunities so the children of former slaves could utilize higher education as the vehicle for moving into mainstream America. Indeed, it can be said that the quality and quantity of the contributions made by HBCU's through the lives of their graduates have far exceeded the expectations of their founders.

This book is not a history of black higher education. Like other American colleges and universities, each black institution has a unique structure, character, mission and history. It is not profitable, therefore to generalize about these institutions as a group. There is, however, at least one common denominator among the private and public black colleges of higher education in this country: they have served as the principal means for inspiring and educating the best and brightest minds of blacks in both the nineteenth and twentieth centuries.

Hampton Normal and Agricultural Institute, as it was known in the early years, has been the flagship for a host of other colleges in the United States as well as in Africa, Japan and the Virgin Islands. For example, Booker T. Washington, Hampton's most renowned graduate, was encouraged by General Samuel Armstrong to go to Tuskegee, Alabama to establish an institution which encompassed the operational model of Hampton Institute. Moving from the nineteenth into the twentieth century, Hampton maintained a stature that was emulated by others. In the decade of the 1980's, Hampton made the transition from a somewhat restricted college to a small comprehensive university. Putting into operation strategies which propelled it into competition with both black and white schools, it received national recognition as an institution with a special vision of higher education.

This contemporary history attempts to show how remarkably, one of America's post-Civil War black schools was able to maintain its standard of excellence during a time when competition for blacks at white colleges and universities had escalated.

The transformation has its roots in the early 1970's when President Jerome H. Holland left to assume the ambassadorship to Sweden. The college was faced immediately with three challenges: (1) interim and short-term presidents, (2) the fallout of student unrest which began in the late sixties, and (3) the aggressive recruitment of superior black students and faculty on the part of white colleges to fulfill the mandate of the 1964 Civil Rights Act.

In 1978 the board of trustees selected a new president to lead the college during what would truly be a transitional period for all of American higher education. During the late seventies, the eighties and into the early nineties, changes in ethnic and racial composition of the student population, economic downturns, declines in the quality of secondary school graduates, and increasing emphasis on technology in society had a significant impact on the dynamics and operation of American colleges and universities. It is noteworthy that during this challenging period for higher education, Hampton experienced phenomenal growth. Student enrollment increased, and so did the number of students entering with high SAT scores and outstanding grades. The college moved to university status, expanding its programs and increasing the quality of the faculty. Equally important, the acquisition of external funds for program enhancement, research and physical improvement accelerated at an unparalleled pace.

My discussion of the administrative, managerial and operational practices and procedures is presented with a great deal of documentary support so that the reader can appreciate better how much impact the various component parts of this institution had in the overall transformation. In order for a university to fulfill its mission, it is necessary for all segments of the infrastructure to work together to maintain a healthy balance or homeostasis toward a common objective--just as the parts of the human body must work in symphony with each other.

The book's cover reflects the melding together of Hampton's glorious past with the current living history of the university. The statue of Booker T. Washington, commissioned in 1984, reflects the leadership and strength of Hampton students and alumni. McGrew Towers, a women's dormitory erected on the waterfront, is a symbol of the new female status. Wilder Hall, a new men's dormitory, is a testimony to the civil rights struggle. Named after Virginia's first black governor, it reminds all of us that one can achieve in spite of adversity. The Olin Engineering Building, funds for which were donated by the Olin Foundation, is a symbol of corporate America's confidence in Hampton University. The William R. and Norma B. Harvey Library is a state-of-the-art facility which will serve future generations of students. As the montage suggests, the various components of the university blend together into a cohesive whole, and that indeed is the operational mode of Hampton University.

In chapter one, I present a capsule of the university's illustrious past. I do not attempt to provide the reader with a comprehensive history of Hampton prior to 1978. One is directed to the work of Dr. Nancy McGhee, writer of the university's history through 1977.

Chapters two and three give the reader a close view of the new president and his leadership style, especially in "selling" Hampton University to parents, students, alumni and influential individuals generally.

In chapter four, I document President Harvey's impact on Hampton University, the local community, Virginia and the nation.

Chapters five, six and seven describe the effect of fund raising on program development while showcasing the success of the administration and faculty in obtaining external funds to support those programs.

Sound fiscal management is no doubt the major factor in the growth of the university during the 14-year period of Dr. Harvey's tenure. A budget surplus for 14 consecutive years and aggressive fund raising have allowed the institution to move rapidly into the forefront of many areas. Chapter eight highlights the fiscal vitality of Hampton University during this period.

There is no place like Hampton University in the eyes of many college-age youngsters. Chapter nine gives some insight into strategies used to attract talented young people to the university as well as support and nurture them while they live on campus.

In chapter ten, I offer an overview of academics in a period which fostered increased commitment to research, innovation and scholarly productivity. The transition of Hampton from college to university was greatly dependent upon the quality of curricula offerings and other faculty activities.

Chapter eleven is a kaleidoscope of various parts of the university.

Finally I have included an epilogue: it consists of responses to a survey instrument on the future of the university.

A GLORIOUS PAST: LEADERS, BUILDINGS, AND EVENTS

When Dr. William R. Harvey assumed leadership, the college had a ready served the nation for 110 years. So its dynamic heritage provided a strong foundation from which the current administrators, faculty, alumni and students could draw. I want to provide a historical overview of that heritage from 1868 to 1977. Some of the data was selected from *Hampton Institute Historic Brochure*, published by Parke Rouse, and *Hampton University Historic Brochure* by Jeanne Zeidler, director of the Hampton University Museum. I am indebted greatly to the university's brochure, *Visions of Our Past* for the information it offers about the significant achievements prior to 1978.

The First President

Hampton Institute was founded by Brigadier Union General Samuel Chapman Armstrong. He was born in Maui in 1839, the sixth son of Rev. Richard Armstrong, a Congregationalist from New England. Samuel Armstrong was sent to the mainland in 1858 to be educated at Williams College under the esteemed Mark Hopkins. Following the Civil War, he was sent to Old Point Comfort, Virginia, by the Freedman's Bureau to help the thousands of blacks who were encamped around Fort Monroe, without homes or jobs. He was determined to start a school for blacks like the Hilo Training School that his father had created for native Hawaiians.

The general begged for money from the American Missionary Society to buy Little Scotland, a farm on Hampton Creek. This became the campus. The society first asked an older man to run the school. When he declined, it turned to Armstrong. The institute that began in 1868 had about 25 students, taught by whites.

For a long time, the institute was not popular with Virginians because the war was too recent, and Yankees were regarded dubiously. The campus was a little world to itself. Although the Armstrongs and other white teachers were snubbed by some locals, the school grew. By 1874 it had $370,000, some of it raised by the student choir singing spirituals and gospel songs in concerts throughout the North.

Samuel Armstrong's faith in the value to the entire society of educating black people has been well documented through the lives of the students who have graduated from the institution. His legacy lives on in the students, faculty, administration and alumni. The alma mater accurately describes the impact of those who have been touched through Armstrong's philosophy:

> *Oh Hampton we can never make you a song*
> *Except as our lives do the singing.*

Samuel Armstrong will never be forgotten. The school he founded is today a prestigious and well-endowed university whose graduates, known around the world, are making a difference. Like his missionary father in Hawaii, Armstrong left his world better than he had found it.

Succeeding the founder have been 10 able, visionary leaders listed below:

Hollis B. Frissell (1893-1917)   **James Gregg** (1918-1929)
George Phenix (1930)   **Arthur Howe** (1930-1940)

Malcolm MacLean (1940-1943)   Ralph Bridgeman (1944-1959)
Jerome Holland (1960-1970)   Roy D. Hudson (1970-1976)
Carl M. Hill (1977-1978)   and currently **William R. Harvey** (1978-)

Buildings Tell a History

Hampton University continues to be a model where individuals of diverse races, cultures, religions, and socio-economic backgrounds work together harmoniously in pursuit of a common goal of building and maintaining an outstanding institution of higher education. Through the generosity of noted philanthropists, trustees, corporate leaders and other contributors to Hampton, one finds an array of impressive buildings including five national historic landmarks on the waterfront campus.

The **Mansion House** is the only building built before 1868 on the Hampton Institute campus. The architecture is Southern Colonial, and the original cost was $3,766, made available by the American Missionary Association. It serves as the residence for the first family and for entertaining official guests of the college.

Memorial Church was built in 1886. The church tower is 150 feet in height and contains a four-faced illuminated clock. The yellow pine pews were built by Hampton Trade School students. J.C. Cady of New York served as architect of the Italian Romanesque structure. Its original cost was $65,000, the gift of the Frederick D. Marquand Estate through Elbert B. Monroe, president of the board of trustees, and Mrs. Monroe.

The **Academy Building** was erected in 1870 and was destroyed by fire in 1879. A second academy, used for classrooms, houses the University Museum, designed by Richard Morris Hunt of New York, one of America's leading architects. The bell outside of the building was used daily to call students to class, meals and daily chapel. It was named Schurz Hall in 1915 in honor of the Honorable Carl Schurz, Secretary of the Interior who was a loyal friend and supporter of the institute.

Virginia Hall, also designed by Richard Morris Hunt, was partly "sung up" by the Hampton Singers in 1874 at a cost of $98,000. The structure was built by students and outside labor. It is the oldest of the women's dormitories. Cleveland Hall, another women's dormitory, was built in 1901 at a cost of $51,973, through funds contributed by former pupils of Charles Dexter Cleveland of Philadelphia. Cleveland Hall was connected to the back of Virginia Hall when built, and therefore was assigned the name, Virginia-Cleveland Hall.

Wigwam, which means a lodge or dwelling, was constructed in 1878 at a cost of $14,700. This dormitory, a gift of friends, was planned by the staff and built by Hampton Institute students. It was originally built to house Native American male students, the first of whom were admitted in 1878.

Among other notable buildings of the pre-Harvey era, the following are particularly worthy of mention.

Winona Lodge, a residence for Native American females, was constructed in 1882. The word "Winona" means older sister. This building was demolished in the 1950's to make room for Twitchell and Davidson Halls.

Ogden Hall, long known as the cultural center in Tidewater Virginia, stands on the Hampton campus in memory of Mr. Robert C. Ogden, a member of the board of trustees from 1874 and president of that body from 1894 until his death in 1914. It is said that he had as much to do with the growth of Hampton as his life-long friend, General Samuel C. Armstrong. The devotion on Mr. Ogden's part, of his time, thought, money, and influence to the type of education to which his friend had given his life is today shown in the success of Hampton.

The **Stone Memorial Building** was constructed in 1882 as a men's dormitory. It was a gift from Mrs. Valerie Stone of Massachusetts in memory of her husband, Samuel Stone. Stone Hall has served a number of purposes at Hampton Institute. In addition to its initial use as a men's dormitory, it houses auxiliary offices.

The **Collis P. Huntington Memorial Building**, erected in 1903, was the gift of Mrs. C. P. Huntington as a memorial to her husband who was a trustee of Hampton Institute. This facility housed the library until January 1992. It has become the home of the University Archives and future home of the University Museum.

The **Marshall-Palmer Hall**, known as the Administration Building, was built in 1882 in honor of General J.F.B. Marshall, first treasurer of Hampton. When the building was enlarged in 1918, the addition was named Palmer Hall in honor of General William Jackson Palmer; funds for the addition and renovation were appropriated from the Palmer Fund through Mr. George Foster Peabody.

Turner Natural Science Building stands today in memory of Dr. Thomas Wyatt Turner, the first black to earn a doctorate degree in botany. Dr. Turner served on the Hampton Institute faculty from 1924-45.

Finally, but not to be omitted from any account of Hampton's history and heritage, there is The **Emancipation Oak.** Over ninety-eight feet in diameter, it was the site in 1863 of the first reading of the *Emancipation Proclamation* to former slaves of Hampton. It is said that Mrs. Mary Peake, daughter of a free colored woman and an Englishman, conducted some of the first lessons for newly freed men and women under the oak.

SIGNIFICANT DATES IN HAMPTON INSTITUTE'S HISTORY

In the course of the history of the university many significant events have occurred. The current trustees, administrative officers, faculty, staff, students and alumni have inherited a significant legacy. Past events serve as reminders to the Hampton family (a term used in referring to faculty, staff, students, alumni and friends of the university) that the rich heritage must be continued. Some of the significant historical dates are noted:

September 21, 1868	Charter granted to Hampton Normal and Agricultural Institute
June 4, 1870	Hampton Normal Agricultural School Incorporated
June 16, 1871	First class graduated of five women and 14 men

March 19, 1872	Hampton Institute received one-third of the "Land Grant Fund" established under the Morrill Act passed by Congress in 1862.
August 20, 1877	First meeting of the National Hampton Alumni Association in Saratoga Springs, New York
April 13, 1878	First American Indian students arrived.
1880	"Shellbanks," a stock and grain farm, was purchased to provide an agricultural laboratory for students and to supply food for the school. Shellbanks is now a part of Langley Air Force Base.
November 23, 1887	Whittier School, a primary day school which in 1879 became a practice teaching site for Hampton students, was dedicated to the poet, John G. Whittier, with whom General Armstrong had been long acquainted. A generous gift from the estate of Frederick D. Marquand made possible a newer model building (the Whittier Training School).
May 12, 1928	First issue of *The Hampton Script* was published.
October 6, 1928	Dedication of Armstrong Field; William E. Lee, a graduate of H.I.'s building construction program drew the plans for the structure, and construction was done by students. The total cost of the stadium was $12,900 ($10,000 of which was donated by alumni).
April 21, 1930	Dr. Nathaniel Dett and choir sang before President Herbert Hoover at the White House.

July 1, 1930	Name changed from Hampton Normal and Agricultural Institute to Hampton Institute; title of "principal" changed to "president"
1931	Kelsey Hall, a dormitory for girls, was a gift from Mrs. Clarence Kelsey in memory of her husband, a former vice chairman of the board of trustees.
April 21, 1932	Hampton Institute accredited by Southern Association of Colleges and Secondary Schools as a "Class B" School
May 31, 1932	First Master's Degree awarded (M.A.)
1932	The George P. Phenix School was erected, a gift from the General Education Board. Phenix School was Hampton Institute's elementary and secondary laboratory which also served as the senior high school for blacks in the city of Hampton until the 1960's.
January 24, 1933	Hampton Institute accredited by Southern Association of Colleges and Secondary Schools as a "Class A" School; Trade School advanced to the college level
May 1933	In a vote conducted by the *Hampton Script*, students chose "Pirates" as the name of the school mascot.
July 8, 1942	U.S. Naval Training School, the first offered at a black college, activated and continued until August, 1945

June 25, 1943	Charles White mural, *The Contribution of the Negro to Democracy in America*, dedicated in Clarke Hall
October 29, 1943	Scrolls presented to 39 charter members of the Quarter Century Club at Convocation
1946	*Hampton Script*, the official student newspaper, received "All American" ratings from the Associated Press (AP).
1950	Entrance gate sign built by Hampton Trade School students and financed by the 1945 and 1949 graduating classes
December 5, 1957	Hampton Institute admitted to the Southern Association of Colleges and Secondary Schools
September, 1962	Establishment of Nongraded Laboratory School
September 16, 1969	Virginia Hall, Academy Building, Mansion House and Memorial Church included in the *Virginia Landmark Register*
September 19, 1974	Fifteen acres of the Hampton Institute campus designated a National Historic District for the historical importance of Virginia Hall, Academy Building, Mansion House, Memorial Chapel, Wigwam, and Emancipation Oak
April 19, 1975	Hampton Institute designated as a National Bicentennial College by the American Revolution Bicentennial Administration

THE NEW PRESIDENT

On Friday, March 24, 1978, it was announced that Hampton Institute's next president would be Dr. William R. Harvey, 37, a vice president of Tuskegee Institute in Alabama.

In July 1978, Harvey assumed his position, and Hampton Institute changed its course. William R. Harvey came with youth, vitality and vision. He began his tenure during a period of transition not only for Hampton, but for all HBCU's. It was the first period in the history of higher education in America that open competition for the best and brightest black students and faculty would occur between black and white colleges. The new president came to Hampton after affirmative action legislation had opened up new opportunities and options for women and minorities in higher education. He came at a time when public trust in higher education was waning, and the corporate sector was questioning the breadth of knowledge and the skill level of college graduates. Harvey's dream was made visible in his inaugural address. He knew what he wanted to do, where he wanted to go, and why he wanted to go there.

An editorial in the *Tuskegee News* by Stan Volt shortly after it was announced that Harvey had been a top contender for the presidency described him as "a quality person, possessing the highest ideals of leadership and administrative ability; a class guy...What a loss to Tuskegee it will be for Bill Harvey to go to Virginia. What a tremendous gain for Hampton Institute."

James J. Henderson, the chairman of the board of trustees, and Dr. Carl Hill, the current president of the college, were elated. Henderson stated that the board of trustees felt that Dr. Harvey, who possessed outstanding credentials, was an excellent choice to continue moving the college toward achieving its established goals.

Dr. Carl Hill, retired president of Kentucky State University and an alumnus of Hampton Institute who served as its president during the two-year period following the resignation of Dr. Roy Hudson, applauded the choice of Harvey as its 12th President. He indicated that the new president was a very fine gentleman, a young, energetic man, and overall an excellent choice to engineer the master plan that had been designed for the institution's development.

At 37, Dr. Harvey was the youngest man to hold the Hampton presidency in post World War II history. As an editorial in the Newport News *Daily Press* put it, "Although 37 does not put a college president in the 'boy wonder' category, it is relatively young. It seems especially young in this case because Hampton Institute is, essentially, a conservatively operated institution. Competition for the post was keen with 140 reported to have applied for the opening."

Dr. Harvey had been vice president for student affairs since 1972 at Tuskegee. He had shown that he could establish rapport with students quickly and therefore be especially effective in urging them to achieve. Using his considerable talents, the new president lost no time before making his expectations known to his Hampton constituency.

"Inferiority is a state of mind; that's what my father used to tell us," Harvey said upon his arrival in the Hampton Roads community. "I believe very strongly in high standards, personally and from an institutional stand point. I believe in high expectations from professors, administrators, and students." In his first speech to a community group, at the First Baptist Church in Hampton, the new president told the congregation, "It has become easier and easier for teachers simply to meet their classes rather than provide a stimulating environment for students to learn. Basic skills are being diminished all over the country, at both white schools and black schools. All kinds of standardized test scores have fallen. We've got people graduating who can't read or write. Folks ought to be made to maintain certain levels and colleges ought to make sure that happens."

Although Harvey favored the traditional practice of black colleges of admitting a percentage of marginal students, he let it be known in this, his first public address, that colleges and universities are not obligated to keep students if they do not measure up to academic standards set by the institution. He continued, "I don't think that colleges ought to acquiesce because the student hasn't reached a certain level of development. Colleges and universities should not gear themselves to their clientele, but vice versa."

A Dream of Excellence

It became apparent from the very beginning of Dr. Harvey's tenure at Hampton Institute that he would need to exhibit unusually strong leadership, enthusiasm and drive if he were to achieve his dream of overall excellence for the institution. He knew that excellence in education required money and that limited monetary resources had always plagued small colleges, historically black private colleges and universities in particular. He began to develop plans for a large fundraising campaign in order to address this basic need.

Strengthening the Financial Resources

The budget deficit of $151,720 at the end of the 1976-77 fiscal year was the most critical problem that the new president had to face. Although Hampton's endowment placed it in a prestigious position, the margin of financial safety was not enough to ensure its future economic security. In an interview with Marvin L. Lake of the *Virginian Pilot and Ledger Star* in June 1978, Harvey indicated that one of his main objectives would be to strengthen the institution's financial condition. "Black institutions have always had to fight the wolf from the door," he declared. "Even Hampton, with a $33 million endowment, has to continue to press for more if we hope to have the kinds of programs that attract good students--white and black--and pay the salaries of top professors."

The new president began with the clear intention of increasing the awareness of the American corporate sector, alumni and faculty of the need to invest in the financial future of the institution. Having come to the university after completing graduate work at Harvard, Harvey was well aware of the level of corporate support, federal grants, estate giving, and alumni support of larger mainstream universities.

In addressing the need to raise the consciousness of corporate America, Harvey said that major corporate heads "will think that they have done well by giving a black college $5,000 to $10,000 where they've given the white college $100,000 to $200,000." While the new president placed fund-raising high on his agenda, he stated early that raising money "is only a means to an end." His purpose was to carry on the mission of Hampton founder General Armstrong of providing strong leadership so that students would continue to have the opportunity to acquire an "education for life" through active "learning by doing."

Establishing the First Agenda

President Harvey quickly established his agenda for the university. Within a month of his official arrival at Hampton, the young president made it a high priority to market Hampton to the corporate sector. Addressing business executives in Hartford, Connecticut, in September 1978, he indicated the unique features of Hampton Institute:

- its demand for high academic standards for all its programs
- the oldest continuous baccalaureate nursing program in Virginia
- its scenic beauty featuring water on three sides, 200 acres of clean, lush, wooded greens and campus buildings of significant charm

- the placement of its students and graduates in top schools and corporations
- its endowment portfolio, which at the time ranked 53rd nationally and first among traditionally black colleges
- the fiscal support of its alumni

Discussing his future plans for Hampton Institute with these business executives, he told them that this "marvelous institution of international acclaim is intricately related to the free enterprise system," and encouraged them to play a role in the future of the institution if they believed that "the most faithful ally in the free enterprise system is the small independent college which by its own operation...supports the same principles of freedom and independence that business and industry seek to protect in their own and the nation's self interest..."

Harvey invited the corporate leaders to join him in investing in the success of Hampton. There were several avenues, in his mind:

- developing a community of interest between their firms and Hampton Institute
- giving gifts for unrestricted purposes or to a specific program;
- arranging for visiting professors to spend a semester or academic year on campus
- participating with the corporate cluster organizations and
- serving on the President's Council or Board

The appeal the new president made to the Hartford group was the first of what was to become Harvey's Hampton University Marketing Portfolio. Fund-raising continues to be a high priority for university presidents at private institutions of higher education and, as a new young president, William R. Harvey took on that responsibility with enthusiasm.

Inauguration: More Than Pomp and Circumstance

It soon became apparent that the 12th president of Hampton Institute was determined to establish an agenda for the college that included involvement in broad societal issues. His agenda was given public exposure through the week-long celebration which culminated with his formal inauguration on Saturday, March 24, 1979.

The week's events opened with a morning church service at Memorial Chapel and an evening of spirituals presented by the College Choir, Symphonic Band and Terpsichorean Dance Troupe. The subsequent events included the following:

- A three-day national conference on the black family (co-sponsored by a group of black judges and the National Alumni of Hampton University)
- A rock concert spotlighting Platinum Hook
- A concert by Lionel Hampton
- A faculty/student art exhibition
- "Interpretation of the Spirituals," a series of lithographs by Ruth Starr Rose
- An African art exhibit
- A dramatic improvisation of the History of Hampton Institute
- A commissioned musical composition, "Hold Fast The Dream," by Roland Carter

During the formal inauguration, Harvey described the future direction of the institution. In his inaugural address the new president sought to unite the past with the present and set his agenda for the future. Harvey's inaugural address became the blueprint for the contemporary history of the university, and is presented in its entirety.

3

THE INAUGURAL ADDRESS OF DR. WILLIAM R. HARVEY
Saturday, March 24, 1979

May I express my appreciation to all of you who are in attendance today. Your presence is an honor to me personally and to an institutional family that is 111 years old. Founded in 1868 by Brevet Brigadier General Samuel Chapman Armstrong, Hampton was established to train former slaves by their living example to "go out and teach and lead." From the beginning, Hampton stressed General Armstrong's concept of "education for life" and "learning by doing." Students learned their lessons about the dignity of labor, the value of self-sufficiency and self-reliance, the appreciation of the value of time by experiencing the act and sensing the satisfaction of achievement. They learned to build character through building buildings on campus and in the community. They learned bookkeeping by keeping their personal ledgers balanced and ready for inspection at all times. They learned to write by writing not only their lessons, but letters of appreciation to friends and donors of the institution.

Hampton's uniqueness has manifested itself from the start in other ways as well. Consider, for an example, the Hampton Museum established in 1868 which is currently recognized as the largest ethnological collection in the state of Virginia and possibly in the entire South and known especially for its African and Indian collections; or the college archives which consist of more than 800,000 original documents and photographs including works of former Presidents James A. Garfield, William Howard Taft, Franklin Delano Roosevelt, as well as Frederick Douglass and Booker T. Washington; or the establishment of the Central Intercollegiate Athletic Conference founded on this campus in 1912; or the Hampton Institute Musical Arts Series which has been in continuous existence for more than half a century and has a history of having brought to the college and its surrounding community the best national and international performing talent available.

These values and indications of uniqueness are as much a part of the Hampton Experience today as they were then. Under this administration, the twelfth of this great college, we shall continue to strive for truth and beauty and excellence in all of the things that we do. We shall emphasize dignity and decency. In curricular and extra-curricular activities, we shall promote the ideals of self-reliance, learning by doing, and the dignity of labor. We shall demand of ourselves and all who are associated with the college high standards and exemplary performance. Emphasizing excellence and high standards is not to be nostalgic about a bygone era, for I (myself) believe in these things and establish them as hallmarks for a continued prosperity. Furthermore, this is the Hampton way. You see, Hampton Institute is more than an educational institution of excellence. It is an institution that has a soul, a tradition of hard work, loyalty, high academic pertinence, warmth, character building, spiritual vigor, and yes, sacrifice. This institutional soul guides us, sustains us and pushes us as we move forward on a daily basis.

Hampton Institute addressed some of these ideals during the week with its inaugural activities. At the Sunday morning inaugural church services, Father Baxter, rector of St. Cyprian's Episcopal Church, challenged the college community to resist mediocrity.

He said that students should be faithful to their capacity to achieve and the sense of purpose related to that achievement. Administrators, he said, must be concerned with more than survival. They must be committed to excellence. Faculty must ignite the classroom with a power, a presence and a purpose. They must challenge and inspire students with their own excellence of skill. This was an inspired message challenging us all to the pursuit of excellence.

The Sunday evening program, "An Evening of Spirituals" by the College Choir, Terpsichorean Dance Troupe, and Symphonic Band, consisting of students, gave a magnificent performance. During the week other students were involved in a dramatic production, art shows, a jazz concert, and a symposium. These outstanding students showcased not only their marvelous talent, but also the rich heritage and cultural strengths that are an intricate part of the Hampton experience.

The First National Conference on the Black Family was another event held at Hampton Institute as a part of the inaugural activities. This was Hampton Institute's way of challenging society--both black and white America--to return to the basics of moral and social decency and to recommit itself both spiritually and financially to restoring the family, which is the microcosm of a nation, to its rightful place as the benchmark of the social order. The conference was inspired by a number of leading black jurists, including Hampton Institute graduate Judge Joseph Williams. "The judges reasoned that strikingly prominent in most of the cases coming before the court was the evident deterioration of the family and probably, as never before, the family's essentially abject surrender of its responsibilities, its prerogatives, its control of its own destiny and that of its children."

The pathological negligence from society further aggravates the situation. Our unemployment and underemployment figures are astronomically staggering; the welfare system has repeatedly proven a failure for reducing our economic dependence on society; the needles of drug abuse are numbing the young and indigent at an epidemic proportion; the penal system which incarcerates our young at an alarming rate has been rendered futile in terms of rehabilitation; our mental and physical health care is abysmal and our youth are being funnelled through the elementary and junior high school systems--particularly in the large and impoverished inner cities--only to later learn that upon entering senior high school they are termed "functionally illiterate."

Therefore, as an academic institution that has historical commitment to turning out good doctors, lawyers, craftsmen, engineers and teachers, we took the opportunity of the Black Family Conference to issue a loud clarion call to Black America. That call is that we must begin to do more for ourselves and the first step is with the family. It is my firm belief that a strong family unit is the greatest source of strength that this nation, or indeed, the world has to offer.

The need for this uniqueness and reliance on self-sufficiency and other proven strengths is just as great today, not only for Hampton Institute, but for our nation and world. The need is so great because the problems are so many.

When we look at our society--or, really, our global village--the problems are large and undeniable. Our double-digit inflation here and sagging dollar abroad force us to rethink our priorities and direction. Economists and social analysts point loudly to an around-the-corner recession, the windfall of which would rival the Great Depression of the 1930's. As an appendage to this, a drastic and crippling food shortage is said to be imminent and already our reservoirs of oil and other energy producers are rapidly depleting. Our nation's dependence upon foreign resources is constantly discussed among scholars and laymen alike and is demanding and receiving greater and more pointed coverage on page one of our newspapers. There are little wars and the rumors of wars in every corner and hamlet of the planet.

Add to this the seeming lack of confidence that we have in our national government. Even after the dramatics of last week's peace mission, the latest public opinion poll does not show an increase in the percentage of people who feel that the President is doing a good job. But the President of this nation is not the only one. Doctors, union leaders, business men, and, yes, college presidents are held up for censure. College presidents received a high confidence score of 33 percent--up 2 points from 1976--but significantly below the 61 percent recorded in 1966.

It is no accident that in these grave days the thoughts of men should turn to religion and to God. We are living through one of the recurrent crises in history that offer a special challenge to the very spirit of man.

We who have rested our security on our mighty weapons; we who have been free from the stark hunger that crushes the spirits of millions of other people;

we who have trusted to our ingenious use of nature to continue an incredible prosperity and high standard of living, now feel ourselves threatened and in a danger that has never before been as close, as real or as uncompromising. We know now that although we might fight, we cannot in the horrible end conquer either what we seek or need. Our weapons are futile against intangible ideas; our statesmen may debate political realities but without conclusion; we talk only of war . . . as if thereby we might still the deep and sickening uneasiness of fear. It is no wonder that man's thoughts turn to religion and to God. It is either this or empty futility.

Students of the *Old Testament* remind us that there have been other such periods when men were stirred by social unrest and strife of classes, by a decline of national morale, by the weary threat of war, military service, the miserable lot of displaced persons in unfriendly countries, and the desperate appeal to God: "Oh that thou wouldst rend the heavens and come down."

We know, too, that the trouble then and now was moral and spiritual decay, and that in the end the decisions to be made are those made in the minds and hearts of the millions of men and women like ourselves.

Whether we like it or not, we are all bound together on this one earth--the rich and the poor, the famous and infamous, the king and the common man, the black and the white--we are inextricably bound. We need God and we need each other.

We are better off here in America when there are no wars in the Middle East. We are the healthiest when all disease has been eradicated. No man should consider himself literate until all men can read and write. None of us are free until all of us are free. Eugene Debs perhaps said it best: "As long as there is a lower class, I am in it. As long as there is a criminal element, I am of it. As long as there is a man in jail, I am not free."

What does this mean to those of us here at Hampton Institute? It means that in our efforts to remain responsive to the special concerns and challenges that each age has presented, we shall emphasize self-reliance, hard work, the dignity of labor, and learning by doing to provide an education for life. To meet this challenge, Hampton will continue to base its forward-looking and innovative posture on its own creative quality and genius of history, tradition and culture. It is this pursuit of excellence and maintenance of high academic pertinence that causes my on-campus colleagues and me to analyze some additional directions for the college. Let me quote from my September 10, Opening Convocation speech when these new directions were proposed.

"First, there ought to be a core of courses that everyone takes. In today's highly technical and sophisticated world, every Hampton Institute student ought to be able to read, write and do basic computations at a certain level. A Hampton Institute student ought to have some knowledge and basic understanding of history, literature and arts. Equally important is the opportunity to do some thinking about ethics and morals. It is my firm belief that decency is as important as degrees, and I want the Hampton students to not only be good doctors, lawyers, professors, engineers and nurses, but I want them to be good moral leaders who have a sense of commitment to community and service as well.

"Secondly, the area of business should be strengthened, particularly in the areas of finance, accounting and management. The stability that should result from such a strengthening will provide the strong basis for moving into an MBA Program. The Hampton MBA would be slightly different than those at other institutions. As a part of the degree requirements, all students would have to experience at least six months or a full semester in the world of work.

"The third area that we are planning for is the establishment of centers for high-level scientific work and research. It is my judgment that the under-representation of minorities in the marine science area and other science areas is a national concern. Therefore, the establishment of centers to develop minority capability in the broad range of ocean resources, marine science, fisheries, maritime law as well as such NASA-related areas as remote sensings, instrumentation, aerodynamics and materials research are under consideration. If this judgment is sound, there is no better or finer institution to do it than Hampton Institute.

"The fourth new area is that of reinstituting a four-year academic program of building technology. This new four-year curriculum will allow students the options of applying their skill directly, teaching in trade or high schools, or perhaps going on to graduate study. The idea is that every college student will not sit behind a desk or work in an office or classroom upon graduation. At Hampton, we continue to believe in the dignity of labor and working with one's hands.

"In addition, we are also planning to expand the continuing education effort so that working mothers and fathers and others may take advantage of the Hampton Institute experiences."

On campus, faculty, staff and student task forces have been working rather assiduously on determining the feasibility of these new directions. As of this date, all of the committees have made their reports to me. All of the reports are favorable, but more than that they have provided a blueprint for making the proposals a *fait accompli*. In the area of marine science, the faculty has approved the curriculum for Hampton to begin offering a degree next year. The other areas are moving ahead in a deliberate yet highly positive fashion.

We can continue to move ahead. We can only do so if we work together, however. With my Hampton Institute colleagues and me working together, and the help and prayers of others, what can be accomplished is limitless.

I accept the challenge, responsibility and privilege of leading this magnificent place we call "Our Home by the Sea." I pray for the wisdom and courage to provide stable leadership while dreaming bold new dreams.

Langston Hughes said:

First in the heart is a dream

Then the mind starts seeking a way ...
Then the hands seek other hands to help
A community of hands to help
Thus the dream becomes not one man's dream
    alone
Not my dream alone
But our dream
Belonging to all the hands who build.

This is my dream, this is my prayer.

THE PRESIDENT'S IMPACT

Like it or not, in the last quarter of the twentieth century, successful college presidents, in order to thrive in the highly competitive economic arena in which colleges found themselves, had to move away from the traditional management style of consensus building that had been the mode of operation in the academy in the early part of the century.

In a comparative study of the styles of 214 college presidents and top executives outside higher education, Grossman (1990, p.35) discovered that those outside of the educational arena do not rely on the consensus-building management model. He found that successful executives "listen carefully to constituents; they provide clear direction, and no one doubts who makes the final decision. Once they decide on a course of action, they do not wait for consensus before moving ahead." This form of management, says Grossman "is more effective when time is of the essence or when one must make a difficult choice that will benefit the whole at the expense of its part."

This is William R. Harvey's management style. While the typical college president sought consensus, Harvey sought to motivate rather than simply steer the institutional "ship." Annual assessments of progress, for example, reflect his creative leadership in transforming Hampton Institute into Hampton University and in propelling it into the mainstream of American higher education.

The First Year

After one year as chief executive of Hampton University, President Harvey gave this assessment:

> *The year 1978-79 was a good one by any measure at Hampton Institute. There were signs that a spirit of community was developing in line with our focus on excellence. There was a widespread renewal of concern for the quality of the Hampton experience, and a commitment to endow the young men and women who came to us with the intellectual capacity to discover and understand factual knowledge, coupled with the capacity to evaluate and discriminate and make choices based on reason.*
>
> *Hampton Institute has many strengths--a good faculty; students eager to learn; an academic program which, while traditional, is flexible; a statement of mission which is responsive to the needs of our students; a balanced budget in 1978-79; a growing interest in Hampton Institute by the corporate sector and an alumni organization which not only contributed $263,000 in 1978-79, but also supported the college in numerous other ways, especially in recruitment. Good teaching has highest priority at Hampton Institute, for we believe our society needs citizens who can lead, who have high personal and moral standards, who are problem-solvers, and who desire to improve the quality of life for their fellowman. We are concerned with providing the best possible environment for learning for the 3,000 students who come to us from diverse backgrounds--both in terms of prior*

learning experiences and geography."

His first years were watched closely by the media, and they responded with enthusiastic reports.

Phil Timp, a local reporter from the *Daily Press* reviewed the president's first year and indicated that when Harvey had became the college's top executive in July of 1978, he was faced with a deficit but had promised a balanced budget in that first year. Hampton Institute completed the year with a $44,000 surplus. The writer also noted that the president credited this success to a hard, tough fiscal management policy as well as to local and national help. Harvey gave special credit to Lucius Wyatt, former vice president for business affairs and treasurer; Eugene Johnson, then financial comptroller, and trustee David Blalock, who was chairman of the fund-raising campaign.

Beating the Odds

In an editorial, a journalist reviewed the status of Hampton Institute in relationship to historically black colleges and universities nationally. He asserted: "With more black students crossing over to predominantly white institutions, it would be conceivable for black colleges to soon go the way of the black high school, black principals, and black teachers." However, he indicated that before one made such an assumption, one should "take a look at Hampton Institute, one of the most renowned of private black colleges in the nation . . . with students pouring in from all over the nation and several foreign countries, the grand old Hampton spirit seems to be saying, 'Happy days are here again.' The trustees of Hampton Institute can look back now with awe and amazement over the miraculous progress the institution has made under the dynamic leadership of its twelfth president, Dr. William R. Harvey. The 1979-80 fiscal year ended with a balanced budget and a 'modest' surplus of $275,000. It seems as though Dr. Harvey has joined hands with alumni, faculty, staff, foundations and corporations and has in two years rebuilt the walls of Hampton Institute."

In 1980, journalist Phil Timp again assessed the management and administrative leadership of the college's president. "Hampton Institute's President, William R. Harvey," stated the reporter, "calls himself a dreamer and lots of people around the country are making his biggest dream come true. In his two years as president, he has travelled extensively--sometimes meeting with eight or more corporations a day in search of money. During his crusades, Harvey stresses that Hampton is a viable educational entity. Harvey stated that he runs the school like a $20 million business. . .'People are becoming more and more aware that we can make an impact. They're not just giving to a black minority cause.'"

National Recognition

Markie Harwood, staff writer for the Newport News *Times-Herald* under the headline "H.I. Realizes 3rd Straight Budget Surplus," contends in his 1981 story that through sound management and aggressive fund-raising, Harvey ended the 1980-1981 year with a $69,000 surplus. This continued success was the result of increased funding from government, private corporations and alumni giving-- and new internal budget management controls. Harwood declared that the Harvey style of leadership had caught the attention of many external governmental, corporate and educational leaders. Harwood further notes, "He was instrumental in the summer of 1981 in the development of position papers that led to an executive order signed by President Reagan to increase the involvement of the nation's 107 historically black colleges in federal programs." When Hampton Institute closed its financial ledger at the end of the 1981-82 year, there was a surplus for the fourth consecutive year.

Responding in 1992 to questions by Harwood about his success, President Harvey said, "There are two sides of the ledger. It's important that we raise money, and it's important that we spend it wisely. If we raise it and don't spend it wisely, we would be frivolous in the eyes of donors. Despite hard economic times, donors see HI as a viable entity. People will support quality."

Hampton's Mystique

Sanders in 1981 said that there is a mystique at Hampton Institute which is shown in the president's ability to attract top students, maintain an annual budget surplus and increase external funding yearly. He attributed part of this mystique to the fact that from the very beginning of his appointment,

> *Dr. Harvey threw himself into the development work of the college with a vengeance. He knocked on corporate doors in New York City from 7:30 a.m. to 5:00 p.m. Before he calls on the corporate chieftains, the Hampton development staff has done its homework. Prior to his visit he knows what the sales of that corporation were last year, how many employees they have, how many Hampton Institute graduates are there, how much money they gave to charitable causes the previous year and what they gave the money to and what the size of their gifts were.*

William Raspberry, noted nationally syndicated columnist, wrote in 1982, "Hampton Institute is doing just fine...while black colleges across America are running scared--wondering whether they can survive Reagan administration cuts in student aid, shrinking enrollments, deficit ridden budgets and the talent drain, as the brightest students and faculty are lured off to white schools--Hampton Institute's young president exudes confidence." He pointed out that President Harvey capitalized on a solid foundation of giving from its alumni who contribute more than any other black college in the country. It also helped, noted Raspberry, that important people have been attracted to the board of trustees like Bill Ellinghaus of AT&T; Virginia Governor Chuck Robb; former Virginia Governor Lindwood Holton; John Duncan of St. Joe Minerals; Jack Dorrand, chairman of Campbell Soups; Sam Pierce, U.S. Secretary of Housing and Urban Development; and actress Elizabeth Taylor--all during Harvey's tenure.

Hampton, An Atypical Success

In June 1982, Marvin L. Lake, reporter for the Norfolk, Virginia *Virginia Pilot*, interviewed individuals on the campus, political leaders, national educators, alumni and trustees in an effort to develop a sense of the Hampton mystique. Lake assessed, "While many of the nation's colleges and universities, both black and white, are plagued by shrinking enrollments and fiscal uncertainties, especially in the wake of federal budget cuts . . .Hampton Institute is enjoying boom times."

Dr. Samuel Meyers, director of the National Association for Equal Opportunity in Higher Education (NAFEO), told Lake that the Hampton success story was atypical. "It's not the picture of institutions generally, black and white," he explained indicating further that many private black institutions were in poor financial shape because they had not engaged in the kind of cost-conscious management that was being practiced at Hampton and because they had not been able to attract the ablest students. Meyers' comments and those of others who were interviewed clearly indicated that other institutions of higher education might do well to emulate the Hampton administrative model.

Harvey attributed the success that resulted in a budgetary surplus of $68,000 during his fourth year to "sound management practices and ambitious fund-raising efforts on the part of many."

Half-way Through a Decade

During his first five years, William R. Harvey carried the Hampton story to alumni groups throughout the country, to corporate board rooms, to the media, and to the White House. Writer Stacey Burling identified him as Hampton's best seller: "He has successfully cultivated the friendship and support of influential Republicans as well as Democrats, a delicate balancing act. Harvey feels free to criticize any of the politicians and believes associating with leaders of both parties is part of his job."

An assessment of the first five years of the tenure of President Harvey reveals unprecedented growth in many areas:

- Five consecutive years of a balanced budget
- Corporate contributions increased by 200%
- Foundation contributions increased by 400%
- Alumni contributions increased by 89%
- Endowment increased from $29.5 to $44 million
- Enrollment increased from 2,734 to 3,837
- SAT scores increased by 93 points
- Thirteen new degree offerings added to the curriculum
- Three new buildings constructed--Marine Science, McGrew Towers and Modular Residence Halls

In assessing his first five years, the president in 1983 noted that there were certain environmental assumptions which guided his operation, among them was his belief "that the wise use of finances is the cornerstone of any successful operational entity." He also operated with the notion that "the rights, interests, and privileges of Hampton Institute take precedence over the rights, interests, and privileges of individual faculty, staff, students, administrators, trustees and alumni. . ."

Harvey promoted team effort; in assessing his first five years, he indicated always that Hampton's success was not entirely due to his individual leadership, but was also due to the work of his administrative cabinet during his first five years. He pointed them out individually:

Dr. Oscar Prater, vice president for administrative services and his colleagues have had an influential role in providing guidance and direction for admissions, recruitment and financial aid. . .During this period we have also maximized the effectiveness of our administrative structure through re-organization. Instead of only departments and divisions, we now have departments, divisions and schools headed by Deans. Under the leadership of **Dr. Martha Dawson**, vice president for academic affairs, our academic program has expanded in quality and quantity.

We have concluded the last five years with a modest surplus. **Mr. Lucius Wyatt**, vice president for business affairs and treasurer, and his colleagues have provided extraordinary efforts to ensure that we operate within our means on a yearly basis...Fund-raising efforts under the direction of **Mr. Laron Clark,** vice president for development have been successful. Hampton was able to increase its corporate giving some 200 percent and its foundation giving by 400 percent! Trustees, alumni, and other colleagues all contributed to this success.

In summing up the first five years, Harvey said, the period under review has been one of excitement, innovation, quality, growth and stability. "As president, I have been fortunate to lead and serve the Hampton Institute community. Yes, we have made immeasurable strides over the last five years, but our work is still unfinished."

The Significance of a Name

With the beginning of the 1983-84 academic year, William R. Harvey moved into the second half of his first decade as president of Hampton Institute. Having achieved a financial surplus every year, Harvey could now give the organizational structure of the college his attention. "Hampton Institute had the structures, facilities, programs, finance and diversified student body required for an undergraduate college, a graduate college and a college of continuing education," he declared.

He asked the Hampton University Board of Trustees to change the name of the college. The recommendation for change had been presented two years earlier by a faculty task force with input from alumni and Board committees.

Mindful of the significant history of the institution, the administration recommended that Hampton Institute continue to be the name of the undergraduate college, that the graduate division become The Graduate College and that the continuing education program be elevated to the status of the College of Continuing Education. Accordingly, Hampton University became the corporate name of the three-dimensional structure.

The name change was more than a formality. It reflected the increased research and national reputation of the faculty, the growth and diversity of programs which had developed within the preceding six years as well as the increased enrollment of students with higher

SAT scores.

After a little over half a decade of growth and financial stability, the president faced the future with a determination to provide the university with an infrastructure that would enable it to move ahead in providing Hampton students with the critical skills, habits and attitudes which would enable them to compete with graduates of America's prestigious universities as well as to enter the global marketplace with confidence.

The Money Magnet

By 1985, William R. Harvey and Hampton University had become nationally known in corporate, educational and governmental circles. In the years ahead the president frequently advised both Presidents Ronald Reagan and George Bush on educational matters. Both Virginia Governors Robb and Wilder sought his expertise in their transitional teams as they assumed office. National and international leaders visited the campus for a firsthand view of how this "politician, academic and fund-raiser extraordinaire," as writer Scott Walsh described him, was successfully guiding Hampton University during a period of recession, if not depression.

Black Enterprise featured William R. Harvey on the cover of its September 1985 issue. The story explored the problems of black colleges and depicted Hampton University as an exception. Writer Derek T. Dingle pointed out that at Hampton University, "financial problems are the least of the administrators' worries. Since Dr. William R. Harvey, 44, graced Hampton's lush green 204-acre campus seven years ago, he became a virtual money magnet for the school, attracting a sizeable amount of support from alumni and corporate donors. In 1985 alone foundations supported grants, which totalled nearly $6.4 million--an amount so massive that the Council for Financial Aid to Education ranked Hampton as the leader under the category of comprehensive master's level colleges and universities." Harvey, according to Mr. Dingle, "Never shies away from an opportunity. . .he solicited proposals from developers nationwide to build commercial properties on a prime 18-acre waterfront tract located on Hampton's campus."

The Maverick President

Scott Walsh, writing in *Portfolio--the Magazine of Hampton Roads,* reasoned that Hampton University President William Harvey's maverick administrative methods were paying off handsomely. He examined the versatility of the president and his impact on the university, noting that Harvey's fund-raising skills had aroused the interest of those in both academic and corporate worlds. In Walsh's view,

> *While some university presidents play down their fund-raising activities as something of a sideshow, Harvey revels in his. He estimates that he spends as much as 70 percent of his time away from campus. But he does not simply go hat in hand to play off the collective guilt of corporate America, or otherwise wheedle and backslap. He approaches the task with all the skill and verve of a corporate takeover specialist. . . .[he] has an easy way about him with nothing of a hustler in evidence. He speaks with great confidence and grace, without embellishing or hedging. He has an uncanny grasp of everything that goes on at Hampton, be it the exact number of artifacts in the school's museum or last year's athletic record. . .*
>
> *By all accounts, Harvey has an acute understanding of the activities and needs of each department. In addition to group meetings, he manages once a week, if only for brainstorming, to meet with each of his five chief officers: vice president for academic affairs, vice president for fiscal affairs and treasurer, vice president for development, vice president for student affairs and vice president for administrative services. Through it all, he minds the budget sheets with a jeweler's eye.*

A Decade of Excellence

Hampton University experienced unparalleled success in the decade from 1978-1988. "While many hands contributed to the success story, the chief executive has the responsibility for whatever happens and does not happen, Harvey said in 1988." The impact of the president on any institution can be measured by the progress or lack thereof during the executive's tenure. An assessment of Hampton University is consequently an assessment of its president.

Hampton University has an impressive history and always is considered "first" among historically black colleges and universities. While Hampton remained dedicated to the mission of its founder--to provide an education for the educationally disenfranchised--the institution in keeping with the political realities of the eighties moved to become a viable institution within the context of mainstream America. In other words, the accomplishments of the first decade under Harvey's leadership must be assessed in terms of the realities of contemporary society. Consequently, this review of Hampton's development during this period is based on criteria that would be used in examining all universities of comparable size and offering, few of which are historically black.

It is noteworthy for any institution of higher education within a decade to:

- Increase its endowment from $29 mil. to $80 mil.
- Undertake a $30 million campaign and generate $46.4 million ahead of schedule
- Increase the student body by 123%
- Increase SAT scores by 187 points
- Expand the museum collection by 24% and increase contributions and grants by 300%
- Balance its budget with a modest surplus for ten consecutive years
- Complete six new buildings--Marine Science, McGrew Towers, Modular Residence Hall, Science and Technology Building, Maintenance Storage facility and the Olin Engineering Building

- Increase applications for admission 293 percent--from 2,404 to 8,720
- Increase faculty salaries 85 percent between 1977 and 1988

Always futuristic in his outlook, President Harvey in his decade report to the board of trustees said, "We still have a great deal to do. We have problems, but more importantly, we have promises. Therefore, with people continuing to work together, Hampton University's future as a striving, dynamic institution is assured."

Fourteen Years Of Presidential Leadership

Now after 14 years of leadership by President Harvey, the institution is perhaps experiencing its most progressive period of development within the twentieth century. Hampton has experienced a period of transition and persistent growth. The already beautiful campus was transformed through the renovation and construction of dormitories, classrooms and other facilities. The most unique addition to the physical plant was the construction of Hampton Harbor, a shopping center and apartment complex built by the university. This is a visionary investment in the future of Hampton University and the Hampton community that assures outside income to support the financial needs of the university. Another significant construction venture was the building of the William R. and Norma B. Harvey Library. This new facility was dedicated on Founders Day, January 1992. The library, as the center of the academic enterprise, includes state-of-the-art, computer-based technology as well as two murals created by the renowned Hampton Institute alumnus John Biggers. The new library stands as the cornerstone of the movement of the university into the twenty first century.

Influence Beyond Hampton University

The reputation of any institution of higher education is enhanced when the president, faculty and other administrators assume highly visible, positive roles in the broader society. Faculty who engage in significant research and share their findings with colleagues at national and international professional meetings increase the prestige of the university. Similarly, when the president of a university is in demand, the institution has increased leverage with funding agencies, governmental institutions and peer institutions. Moreover, the enhanced recognition increases the professional opportunities and achievements of all constituent groups within the university.

William R. Harvey continues to be sought after as a consultant, speaker, guest, board member and advisor to diverse institutions including both the State House in the Commonwealth of Virginia and the White House in the nation's capital. His service is significant not only for his own professional image but also for that of the faculty and the university as a whole. President Harvey's role in "high places" has certainly created global visibility for the entire university.

The president has served diverse groups and has opened doors for others associated with him. A sampling of his leadership in service to the broader community listed below clearly documents the president's impact not only at Hampton University but throughout the community, state and nation.

Significant External Appointments and Honors
1978-1992

Corporate Boards and Foundations

- United Virginia Bank - Executive Committee
- Newport News Savings Bank
- Virginia Foundation for Research and Economic Education

City, State and Federal Appointments

- U.S. Commission on Presidential Scholars
- Fund for the Improvement of Postsecondary Education
- Virginia Education Forum

- Peninsula Economic Development Council - Executive Committee
- Peninsula United Way
- Peninsula Chamber of Commerce
- U.S. President's National Advisory Council
- ESEA - Vice Chairman
- Department of Defense Advisory Committee on Women in the Service

Higher Education Boards and Organizations

- Glenmede Trust Education Advisory Board
- Board of National Merit Scholarship Corporation
- Board of Visitors - University of Virginia
- American Council on Education - Commission on Leadership Development and Academic Administration
- Board of Trustees, Knoxville College
- Alumni Council, Harvard University Graduate School of Education
- Harvard Cooperative Society
- Air University Board of Visitors

Special Leadership Positions and Honors

- Peninsula Chapter of National Conference of Christian and Jews Citation Award
- Honorary Ph.D., Salisbury State University
- Honorary Ph.D., Medaille College
- Honorary Ph.D., Lemoyne-Owen College
- Virginia Laureate Recipient 1992

Recognitions of the Hands That Help to Build

The transformation of Hampton Institute/Hampton University during the period from 1978-1992 is without question the result of the leadership of President William Harvey. However, he continues to share credit for the success of the institution with others. He seizes every opportunity in some way to give recognition to individuals who are making a contribution to society. Likewise he uses every opportunity available to show appreciation to those behind the scenes, many who are not visible to the media or in the limelight. His recognition of these important people is demonstrated in many ways: letters of recognition, announcement at faculty meetings, merit increments and monetary rewards.

Presidential Citation to Community Leaders

Beginning with his first Founders Day in 1979, Harvey established the Presidential Citation Award. The award recognizes individuals who have made society a better place for others. The awards are given to individuals of diverse racial backgrounds, both those in public positions and outside of public domain. Here is a list of recipients.

RECIPIENTS OF THE PRESIDENT'S CITIZENSHIP AWARD

YEAR	RECIPIENT	POSITION
1979	Mr. Gordon B. Cutler	Retired Banker
	Mrs. Ann Kilgore	Former Hampton mayor and councilwoman
	Dr. Flemmie P. Kittrell	Member, H.I. board of trustees
	Mr. Henry "Hank" E. Parker	Treasurer, state of Connecticut
	John H. Sengstacke	President, Robert S. Abbott Publishing Company

1980	Mr. Thomas P. Chisman	President and general manager, WVEC Television, Inc., and trustee, Eastern Virginia Medical Foundation
	Dr. G. Robert Cotton	President, Cedar Knoll Rest Home, Cotton Investment Company, and Cotton & D. Transportation, Inc.; trustee of Hampton Institute and member of the State Corrections Commission of Michigan
	Mrs. Hattie McGrew	Oldest living alumna of Hampton Institute
	Mrs. Jessie M. Rattley	Member, Newport News City Council and president, National League of Cities
1981	Mr. Lawrence P. Barbour,	Manager and proprietor, Barbour's Business Service
	Mr. Herbert V. Kelly, Jr.	Attorney, Jones, Blechman, Woltz and Kelly
	Mrs. Rosa Parks	Civil rights leader

	Mrs. O'Marie N. White	Executive director, Development Programs for the City of Hampton
	Dr. Stephen J. Wright	Former president of Fisk University; former dean of faculty, Hampton Institute, and educational consultant
1982	Mrs. Helen Alexander	Secretary, office of the vice president for academic affairs, Hampton Institute
	Mr. James Alton Cotton	Former postmaster at Hampton Institute and supervisor of the academic regalia department
	Mr. F. Edward Harris	President, United Virginia Bank
	Mr. W. Edgar Nicholson,	Civil rights activist and retired businessman
	Dr. Milton A. Reid	Minister, businessman and editor, *Journal and Guide*
1983	The Rev. Seymour Gaines	Minister and civic leader
	Mr. Thaddeus Stevens Madden	Coach, sportsman and maker of men
	Mrs. William R. Van Buren	Patron of the arts, civic and cultural volunteer

1984	Joseph R. Briggs	A current student who is held in high esteem by his peers and others
	Mr. Henry Clay Hofheimer, II	Outstanding citizen of Norfolk in business, economic and industrial development, banking, real estate and insurance
	Mrs. Pocahontas T. Jackson	Former educator and retired businesswoman
	Mrs. Rachel B. Noel	Retired consultant on community relations, distinguished college professor, outstanding civic and education leader, and former chairman of the board of regents of the University of Colorado
1985	Mrs. Ellen L. Bolling	A volunteer in civic, educational and religious organizations of the Hampton community
	Mr. Sylvius S. Moore	Outstanding swimming coach, former director of physical education and athletics at Hampton University, and holder of the Lindback Distinguished Teaching Award

	Hon. Nelson T. Overton	Judge, 8th Judicial Circuit Court of Virginia
	Mr. Walter S. Segaloff	President, Virginia Specialty Stores, Inc.
1986	Hon. Richard M. Bagley	Member of the House of Delegates, Virginia General Assembly (1965-1985)
	Mr. and Mrs. Harold A. Brauer, Jr.	Co-chairs of the 375th anniversary of the City of Hampton
	Mrs. Alveta Ewell	Anchor for WVEC-TV 13 News
1989	Mr. Joseph W. Gilliard	Professor Emeritus, Hampton University and an outstanding ceramist
	Dr. William P. Magee, Jr.	Surgeon and dentist, and co-founder of the medical mission Operation Smile
	Mrs. Kathy S. Magee	Nurse and social worker, and co-founder of the medical mission Operation Smile
1990	Ms. Barbara Forst	Founder and president of CINEBAR Video Productions Inc.
	Mr. Knox W. Tull	Humanitarian

1991   Mr. Richard Hassell   Founder and sole
                                operator of the Christian
                                Action Organization

       Mrs. Midge Johnston Eason   Community leader and
                                   volunteer

       Mr. Raymond G. Washington   Assistant superintendent
                                   for elementary education
                                   and personnel for the
                                   City of Hampton

Merit Salary Increments

Hampton University as a small college has had to compete with much richer public institutions to maintain competitive salaries. However, with the available resources the president has assisted the academic administration by allocating monies in the annual budget for merit salary increments beyond the basic yearly increment. Faculty members who demonstrate innovative and effective teaching, who secure grants and research funds, or who bring recognition to themselves and the university through other scholarly pursuits receive merit salary increments. Exemplary support staff are also included in the merit program. Staff merit increments are given to those who make special contributions beyond that required or expected.

Christmas Bonus

From 1979-1991 President Harvey was able not only to balance the budget, but to end each year with a budget surplus. The university community and the board of trustees were always proud of that stellar accomplishment. The president was quick to point out to the trustees that his success in securing grants and in effectively managing resources was due in large part to the leadership of selected faculty members, deans and his administrative team. He then gained board approval to give tangible recognition to these faculty and staff with the surplus.

In those years when the surplus was modest, each full-time person received a gift for the family before leaving for the Christmas vacation. In years when there was a significant surplus, faculty received a holiday bonus check, which was either a percentage of one's salary or a uniform amount.

Additional Rewards

In addition to the Christmas bonuses, departments and schools had the option of submitting requests for updating equipment or introducing an innovation. Further, they could secure special fiscal allotments beyond their budget at the end of the academic year from funds resulting from the budget surplus.

The president gave modest monetary awards of appreciation periodically to faculty and staff. Supervisors, vice presidents and deans have requested on occasion that a check be given to those individuals who had made special contributions to the university.

Special Staff Recognition

On the Monday following commencement, a special luncheon is hosted by the president for secretaries, buildings and grounds personnel, and other support staff. At the luncheon, individuals are recognized for years of service. However, the highlight of the luncheon is a drawing in which the winner receives an all-expense paid vacation to Disney World or the Caribbean. In addition, the president permits the support staff to leave early in recognition of the hard work they put into making commencement a success.

The recognition of team effort is one of the best indications of the interpersonal skills of President Harvey. While considered a hard task master, he has also earned the reputation of being a humane administrator and an extraordinary leader. William R. Harvey can be considered a classic contemporary leader.

Summary

Warren Bennis, (1990) a leading authority on executive management, has indicated that "to survive in the 21st Century, we are going to need a new generation of leaders, not managers." He points out that there are crucial differences between managers and leaders:

- The manager administers; *the leader innovates.*
- The manager is a copy; *the leader is an original.*
- The manager maintains; *the leader develops.*
- The manager focuses on systems and structure; *the leader focuses on people.*
- The manager relies on control; *the leader inspires trust.*
- The manager has a short-range view; *the leader has a long-range perspective.*
- The manager asks how and when; *the leader asks what and why.*
- The manager has his eye on the bottom line; *the leader has his eye on the horizon.*
- The manager accepts the status quo; *the leader challenges it.*
- The manager is the classic good soldier; *the leader is his own person.*
- The manager does things right; *the leader does the right thing.*

William R. Harvey embodies the leadership traits depicted by Warren Bennis. His influence is seen in the growth of the university's academic affairs, business and fiscal affairs, development, student affairs, alumni affairs and administrative services.

5

A NEW ACADEMIC MODEL

Prior to the 1980's most faculty felt that being an effective teacher was their only responsibility. Only if especially inclined would a faculty member apply for federal and private funds either for research or for an innovative project. Fund raising was thought to be the responsibility of the president and professionals in the office of development. Those efforts would take away from the basic teaching role of faculty. Many voiced the opinion that Hampton was a teaching college. In the past, the internal review system for promotion and tenure had not recognized the triad of teaching, research and scholarly pursuits, and significant service. For decades faculty had devoted most of their energies to teaching and service to students.

Now in the 1980's, the challenge faced by top academic administrators was changing the institutional mindset to include research and scholarship while *continuing to support the faculty's commitment to teaching and student service.* This challenge was vigorously undertaken by all administrators at the university. Specific strategies were designed to motivate and assist faculty in expanding their roles. This new mindset was to include research and publication efforts and the generation of proposals to support research and program development.

Developing Networks

During the 1979-80 academic year, Martha E. Dawson, the first vice president for academic affairs was appointed. This administrative officer immediately established a networking cabinet identified as the Academic Leadership Team (ALT). The group of school deans and the directors of the library and museum met with the vice president on a weekly basis.

By working collectively, ALT provided the basis for moving departments and schools into the mainstream of higher education through increased efforts in research and grantsmanship.

Deans' Responsibility

"The dean is to be responsible for generating external funds to cover one-third of the operating budget of the school," announced President Harvey in 1984, when the divisions became schools and directors became deans. Deans now had the responsibility of assisting faculty as well as taking a leadership role themselves in fund raising. In general, the president expected that one-third of the operating cost of the university was to come from student fees; one-third was to be generated by academic units, and the final third through the efforts of the president and the office of development. Clearly, innovations and growth required further fund raising; therefore, the president, vice president for development and vice president for academic affairs worked as a team to provide potential grant writers with a coordinated support system for securing external funds.

Technical Assistance

The dean of the graduate college was also appointed assistant vice president for research. This assistant vice president monitored the grant proposal submission process as part of the office of the vice president for academic affairs. Potential proposal writers submitted an "Intent to Submit A Proposal" form to the assistant vice president for research, who reviewed the document and provided technical assistance at the exploratory phase. When the actual proposal writing began, the director of federal grants or other professionals in the office of the vice president for development provided technical assistance to the grant writer. Additionally, consultants with special expertise were often available to the faculty in designing competitive research proposals and institutional grant proposals.

Adjustments in Teaching Load

Faculty at Hampton University carry an undergraduate teaching load that is generally higher than that of faculty at a research university, and they are not likely to have the benefit of experienced graduate assistants. An attempt was made to assist those faculty members who needed time to pursue research or other scholarly objectives by granting them one-quarter released time. Academic deans were able to request released time for research and development through the vice president for academic affairs.

External and Internal Consultants

External consultants were brought in to conduct proposal-writing workshops for schools or groups of individuals through the office of the vice president for academic affairs. A second approach involved the use of faculty members at the university who had established a track record in publishing, research and grantsmanship to conduct proposal-writing workshops. These interdisciplinary sessions stimulated interest among faculty from diverse backgrounds. Following these workshops, the internal consultants served as mentors to proposal writers and provided technical assistance when needed.

Annual Increments for Scholarly Pursuits

Each year the president asked the vice president for academic affairs to identify for merit pay those faculty who had successfully secured a funded grant or received recognition for research or other scholarly activities. The deans in each school established guidelines consistent with their school mission which were then applied when recommending the salary increment for individuals. Therefore involvement in sponsored programs was recognized in a very tangible way.

Recognition for Promotion and Tenure

Perhaps the greatest stimulus to expanding faculty's role in research and grantsmanship was the value placed on these activities in the promotion and tenure process. The documentation of publications in refereed journals and the recognition of ability to secure external grants became a critical requirement for promotion at all levels, and became mandatory for tenure. Evidence of scholarly research and grantsmanship became equated with documentation of effective teaching as means for furthering one's career. The recognition which faculty received from their colleagues and the external community of scholars within their respective disciplines served as stimuli for greater involvement in grantsmanship.

With a review and reward process which provided monetary merit increments as well as recognition in the promotion and tenure process, faculty attitudes changed and Hampton moved into an era where research and grantsmanship became the rule rather than an exception.

University Teamwork

The Hampton University model is a classic example of how a team approach can be used to change faculty attitudes toward externally funded and sponsored programs in a small university. The significant increase in the submission of grant proposals to external agencies was accomplished through cooperation and teamwork among professionals in the office of development, school deans, chairs and faculty members. The coalition that was developed among the vice president for business affairs and treasurer, the vice president for development and the vice president for academic affairs enabled faculty to pursue proposal writing and research without administrative entanglement.

Successful Fund Raising in an Era of Economic Decline

To maintain their solvency, private institutions of higher education depend on the generosity of corporations and philanthropists as well as federal grants and private contributions. Historically black colleges and universities have seldom had graduates who became CEO's of "Fortune 500" corporations. Nor have they had alumni who have amassed the resources to bequeath millions of dollars to the university's endowment. Further, they generally lack the political clout to influence agencies and individuals who are decision-makers in the federal grantsmanship arena. The point then, is that even the successful procurement of relatively small grants at a historically black college is a mark of distinction and a credit to those responsible.

The success of Hampton University faculty and administrators in the period of economic decline that occurred in the eighties and early nineties is indeed phenomenal. Much of Hampton's success in acquiring external funds was a result of strategic planning and aggressive fund-raising initiatives on the part of President William Harvey and Laron Clark, Jr., vice president for development. This duo developed a fund-raising action agenda that resulted in the most successful fund-raising campaign in the history of the university.

In addition to the successful orchestration of a major fund-raising campaign, they used the Hampton University story to inspire alumni, philanthropic foundations, corporate America and private donors to make significant contributions to the university.

The following overview of fund raising during the period from 1978-1990 presented by Laron Clark, Jr. in April 1992 reflects the confidence that the public had in the president, administration, faculty, staff and students of Hampton University.

FUND RAISING AT HAMPTON UNIVERSITY, 1978-1990

A milestone was reached in private foundation support in 1979-80, as the dollars raised from foundations increased from $242,292 the previous year to $667,757. This amount represented a 180 percent increase in new dollars generated from foundations. Selected foundation grants came from these organizations:

Pew Memorial Trust	$250,000
Aetna Life and Casualty Foundation	150,000
Andrew W. Mellon Foundation	150,000
Charles Stewart Mott Foundation	125,750
The Bush Foundation	87,250

Private giving to Hampton reflected an overall increase of $564,055 in new money raised over the previous year. A total of $381,660 was contributed by corporations to Hampton during 1979-80, representing an 11 percent increase over corporate giving during the previous year. A corporate relations function was created within the office of development, thereby increasing the number of individuals making visits to corporations. Both the number of visits to corporations and the number of proposals presented to corporations increased. These visits were up by 40 percent over the previous year, with the gain in proposals submitted rising by 30 percent.

The alumni contributed $341,911 to the Alumni Annual Fund and an additional $85,002 for special purposes. Total alumni giving was $426,913 in 1979-80. A significant rise in alumni giving can be attributed to The Bush Foundation Alumni Challenge Grant which provided a matching incentive for new donors and new dollars.

Fiscal Year 1980-81

For the third consecutive year, using 1978 as the base year, corporate contributions to Hampton continued to show substantial increases. Corporate contributions totaled $461,191 for the year ending June 30, 1981. The overall monies raised in cash and pledges far exceeded that which was received during 1979-80. For example, International Business Machines committed $200,000 to Hampton in the form of a pledge, paying only $40,000 (the first installment) in 1980-81. Xerox Corporation pledged $30,000 and made a $10,000 first installment payment during this period.

The fact that corporate contributions continued to increase dramatically and the fact that corporate contributions increased by more than 100 percent in three years showed a combination of effective short-term efforts involving immediate opportunities for gift solicitation and long-term activities incorporating planning, cultivation and organization necessary to expand the range of private giving to Hampton.

In 1980-81, selected major gifts received by Hampton included:

International Business Machines	$200,000
Charles Stewart Mott Foundation	141,600
Lilly Endowment	149,706
The Bush Foundation	147,000
Alfred P. Sloan Foundation	100,000
Morgan Foundation	50,000

Fiscal Year 1981-82

In 1981-82, gifts from private foundations increased by 53 percent to $885,000. The institution received a total of $249,000 from private foundations in 1977-78--the baseline year. Over this three-year period, gifts from foundations have increased by nearly 400 percent.

Corporate gifts to Hampton increased by 32 percent in 1981-82. During this fiscal year, corporate giving totaled $608,000. In comparison to other institutions of higher education in Virginia, Hampton ranked fifth in 1981-82 in terms of level of corporate gifts received. In rank ordering, Virginia Polytechnic Institute, University of Virginia, University of Richmond and Virginia Military Institute, respectively, placed ahead of Hampton. In a study of corporate support that rated institutions by the amount of dollars received, Hampton ranked 77 in the nation among all institutions in 1981-82. Four years before, 1977-78, Hampton received $223,000 in corporate gifts. Since 1977-78, corporate giving to Hampton increased by about 200 percent.

Alumni contributed $437,000 to Hampton in 1981-82.

Fiscal Year 1982-83

Private giving to Hampton in 1982-83 increased by 14 percent for a net gain of $336,413 in new money. A total of $936,151 was raised from private foundations in 1982-83, representing a six percent increase over the previous year.

Corporate giving increased by five percent to a total of $637,462 in 1982-83. In addition to this total, a corporate grant of $100,000 was received toward the purchase of computer equipment.

Some major gifts and pledges to the capital campaign in 1982-83 included:

The Bush Foundation	$1,250,000
Pew Charitable Trust	900,000
Kenan, Jr. Charitable Trust	375,000
Kresge Foundation	300,000

Sun Company 300,000
Philip Morris 100,000

Alumni contributions were $391,000 in 1982-83, reflecting a slight decrease from the previous year. It was during this period that forming a separate alumni corporation became an issue.

Fiscal Year 1983-84

Gifts to Hampton University from private sources were $3,125,222 for the fiscal year ending June 30, 1984, representing an increase of 14 percent over contributions of the previous year or $395,121 in new money.

Corporate gifts totaled $860,582 in 1983-84, for a new money gain of $223,120 over 1982-83. Contributions from private foundations were up by 45 percent in 1983-84, totaling $1,361,804.

By any objective analysis, 1983-84 was a year of sound achievement in fund raising at Hampton. Selected gifts and pledges were as follows:

Andrew W. Mellon Foundation	$350,000
General Motors Corporation	250,000
Arthur Vining Davis Foundations	75,000
Delta Sigma Theta Sorority	50,000
United Virginia Bank	50,000
Financial Corporation	25,000

Fiscal Year 1984-85

For the seventh consecutive year, private gifts reflected an increase in dollars generated. Gifts from private sources (excluding pledges) totaled $3,125,222 in 1983-84. In 1984-85, $4,227,172 were raised among private sources. In total gains, private giving increased $1,101,950 or 35 percent over contributions for 1983-84.

Corporations contributed $994,258 to Hampton University this year. There was a new money gain of $136,676 in contributions from corporations in 1984-85. Over a six-year period coming into 1984-

85, corporate gifts increased by more than 235 percent. The additional 16 percent increase in 1984-85 established an annual compounded growth rate of 36 percent.

Private foundations contributed $2,166,820 to the university in 1984-85. Gifts from private foundations were up by 59 percent in 1984-85, for a new money gain of $806,016. During the period 1978-1984, a 445 percent increase occurred in gifts generated from foundations. When this gain is added to the 59 percent increase experienced in 1984-85, an annual compounded growth rate of 72 percent was reflected, or a cumulative gain of 504 percent.

Fiscal Year 1985-86

Private gifts to Hampton University (excluding pledges) amounted to $2,348,371 for the fiscal year ending June 30, 1986. Moreover, some $3.3 million were received in pledges during the same period, making total private giving $5,648,371 for 1985-86. In 1984-85, private giving totaled $4,227,172 in cash and another $1,128,692 were generated in pledges, aggregating $5,355,864. When all gifts (cash and pledges) are taken into account, an increase of $292,507 was realized in giving in 1985-86.

As the major activities of the $30 million campaign were winding down, private giving reflected a concomitant decrease in cash received. The decrease in private giving is accounted for in the fact that (1) several major pledges to the campaign ended with the 1984-85 payments and (2) efforts were being made to condition large donor prospects for gift opportunities in the next campaign.

Fiscal Year 1986-87

The university experienced excellent responses to its fund-raising solicitations. Gifts and grants from private sources totaled $3,731,822 in 1986-87. For the same period of 1985-86, a total of $2,347,621 was raised among private sources.

Contributions from private sources reflected an appreciable gain over the dollars raised during the previous year. In fact, private giving rose by 58 percent, representing $1,304,072 in new money.

Gains were experienced in dollars received from all constituent categories. Corporate gifts, for example, rose by 45 percent. A total of $1,017,003 was raised in the corporate sector during this fiscal year.

The following selected major gifts were received during this period:

American Telephone and Telegraph Foundation	$124,000
General Electric Foundation	100,000
William Randolph Hearst Foundation	100,000
General Mills Foundation	60,000
Chesapeake and Potomac Telephone Company	45,000
Rockefeller Foundation	41,000
Culbro Corporation	25,000
Lettie Pate Whitehead Foundation	23,000

Fiscal Year 1987-88

Gifts from private sources (excluding pledges) for 1987-88 totaled $4,785,440. In real gains, private giving increased by $1,053,622 in new money over contributions for 1986-87. The fund-raising results for 1986-87 were up by 28 percent as private giving reached a level of $3,731,822, excluding pledges.

Foundation gifts to Hampton totalled $2,746,310 during 1987-88. Foundation gifts rose by 272 percent in 1987-88. Selected private gifts included:

F.W. Olin Foundation	$828,000
Howard Hughes Medical Institute	600,000
The Bush Foundation	390,000
Booth Ferris Foundation	150,000
Philip Morris Companies	100,000

It is significant to note that contributions from friends increased by 30 percent in 1987-88. A total of $206,568 was contributed by friends, for a gain in new dollars of $48,599. This increase came on the heels of a 125 percent rise in 1986-87 when gifts from friends totaled $157,568.

Fiscal Year 1988-89

Private fund raising has been a major priority at Hampton University for the past eleven years. The extra effort in fund raising paid off during 1988-89, as the institution had a particularly fruitful year. Gifts from private sources totaled $3,796,047 for that fiscal year. The fiscal year total is derived from cash received, as pledges are not included. A total of $2,002,707 was generated from foundations, and our corporate fund-raising activities resulted in an aggregate of $621,562.

Major gifts received included: Charles A. Dana Foundation, $200,000 and Philip Morris Companies, $100,000.

The Alumni Annual Fund generated $468,852 during 1988-89. A special telephone solicitation was conducted among alumni in April, 1989. The Phonathon was designed to solicit gifts from alumni non-contributors. One of the Phonathon's goals was to educate this segment of the alumni population about the value of supporting Hampton University. It is planned that the Phonathon become a regular device in soliciting our alumni.

Fiscal Year 1989-90

Gifts from private sources totaled $3,801,352 for the fiscal year ending June 30, 1990. A total of $2,004,783 was received from private foundations. Corporations contributed $643,056 during this fiscal year. Some highlights of major gifts are listed:

Teagle Foundation	$360,000
Amoco Foundation	250,000
The Ford Foundation	175,000
American Telephone and Telegraph Foundation	150,000
Booth Ferris Foundation	150,000

David and Lucille Packard
Foundation   105,000
Independence Foundation   100,000

Thirty Million Capital Campaign (1982-1986)

In the early 1980's, a $30 million capital campaign was approved by the board of trustees. The five-year campaign was planned to raise funds for endowment, program enrichment, salaries, and construction and renovation. The capital campaign was led by William Ellinghaus, President of American Telephone and Telegraph Company and a member of the board of trustees. Joining Mr. Ellinghaus on the Capital Campaign Steering Committee were trustees David Blalock, G. Robert Cotton, John Dorrance, John Duncan, O.G. Taylor, and Robert Upton.

The campaign was designed to strengthen Hampton, to enhance the quality of its educational program, and to increase the institution's role in higher education. The campaign funding goals are charted below:

Construction and renovation $15 million
Endowed faculty chairs   5 million
Endowed scholarships   5 million
Program enrichment   3 million
Salary improvement   2 million

The $30 million campaign was concluded on June 30, 1986, at which time $46.4 had been generated in cash and pledges. The campaign, the largest fund raising undertaking in Hampton's history, was completed ahead of schedule and exceeded the goal by more than 50 percent. The two largest gifts from private sources were from the Kate Macy Ladd Fund and the F.W. Olin Foundation in the amounts of $7.5 million and $4 million, respectively. Other seven-figure gifts included $2.25 million from the Federal Aviation Administration and $1.25 million from The Bush Foundation.

FACULTY LEADERSHIP

With the guidance of Joyce Taylor, director of federal relations, faculty in all areas of the campus became aware of the grant opportunities in the federal sector. The success rate of individuals and proposal-writing teams ushered in a new era at the university.

While there were more opportunities in some disciplines than in others, all academic units pursued the grant-writing path to initiate new programs and to strengthen existing curricular development. An array of diverse grants was received during the 1980's--into the nineties as well.

The diversity of funded grants greatly enhanced the academic programs and research activities of faculty and students. Many of the initiatives broadened not only the focus of departments and schools, but also the influence of the university far beyond the boundaries of the campus.

Transforming Pure and Applied Sciences

For one unit in particular--the School of Pure and Applied Sciences--external funding became a catalyst in expanding its mission. Dean Robert Bonner was quick to point out that during the previous five years (1987-1992) the School of Pure and Applied Sciences had made significant progress in setting up new programs in concert with Hampton's new university status.

According to Bonner, grantsmanship not only changed the direction of the school, but also stimulated increased research activity at the departmental level, especially projects which include both undergraduate and graduate students. Further, the multidisciplinary clusters which developed drew upon talents in diverse departments. According to Bonner, the departments of biological sciences, chemistry, computer science, engineering, marine and environmental studies, mathematics and physics have been able to take advantage of the opportunity to contribute to areas of research that are highly visible at the national level. Research efforts in the school included these areas:

- Biotechnology developments
- Computer modeling
- Energy conversion
- Environmental studies (pollution and hazardous waste materials)
- Materials science
- Nuclear physics
- Photonics

Bonner noted that the university was well on its way toward the acquisition of important pieces of equipment to support specific projects in broad categories of research. The changes within the School of Pure and Applied Sciences clearly indicate that successful grantsmanship can make a significant difference in the quality and scope of an academic unit.

Strengthening the Research Infrastructure

According to Dr. Demetrius Venable, assistant vice president for research and dean of the graduate college, specific research grants within the science areas were instrumental in assisting Hampton University in the enhancement of its science offerings and the development of high quality research programs.

Venable points out that an excellent example of the impact of grantsmanship on research capabilities is the award to the department of physics titled "Local Effect of Partly Cloudy Skies on Solar and Emitted Radiation" funded in 1980 for three years. According to Venable, "This was the first research grant developed as a joint effort by members of the physics department that had as *one of its principal goals the strengthening of the research infrastructure of the department*."

Funding for the project was a direct result of President Harvey's interaction with administrators at National Aeronautical and Space Administration (NASA) and of his discussion of the importance of the support of such infrastructure in building research activities at HBCU's. The grant, which was funded for over $125,000 per year for three years, allowed the department to purchase state-of-the-art research computers and instrumentation and to hire full-time research assistants, as well as provide direct support for student researchers.

Research conducted under this grant also led to additional long-term NASA grants within the department such as "The Direct Solar Pumped Iodine Laser," "Advanced Solar Energetics," "The Spaceborne Photonics Institute," and the "Research Center for Optical Physics," which was funded in 1991 for a total of $8,500,000 for five years.

Another example of a grant that established research trends within the sciences at Hampton is the National Science Foundation-funded project entitled "Theoretical Intermediate Energy (Nuclear/Particle) Physics Group."

This grant written in 1987 was, in Venable's words, "instrumental in the establishment of a research effort in intermediate energy nuclear physics and established nuclear physics as one of two prime research areas in the department of physics." The faculty research group involved in this project established the university's linkage with the Continuous Electron Beam Accelerator Facility in Newport News, Virginia, which led to significant additional funding in both educational and research efforts. The grantsmanship activities of faculty in the department of physics culminated in 1991 with the establishment of the Nuclear/High Energy Physics Research Center of Excellence funded by the National Science Foundation in the amount of $5,000,000 for a five-year period.

As an outgrowth of the numerous successful research activities of faculty in the department of physics, the university initiated, in 1989, the process that led to the State Council of Higher Education and Southern Association of Colleges and Schools granting approval for Hampton University to award the Ph.D. degree in physics.

Preparing Tomorrow's Researchers

According to Dr. Isai Urasa, chair of the department of chemistry, research activities increased significantly between 1982 and 1992. Within this period the faculty in the department of chemistry succeeded in generating competitive research grants totalling approximately $3,000,000 from such agencies as the National Science Foundation, the U.S. Environmental Protection Agency, the National Institutes of Health, the Department of Energy, National Aeronautic and Space Administration, and the U.S. Coast Guard. Grants came as well from private companies including the Jeffries Trust Fund and the Upjohn Pharmaceutical Company. He also indicated that this external support significantly increased the number of students selecting chemistry as a major, and even increased the percentage of superior students.

Through aggressive proposal writing by the faculty in the department of chemistry, funds were generated to purchase much of the instrumentation needed in analytical chemistry research and training as well as to support graduate students. These resources supported the outstanding research conducted by the faculty in the department of chemistry and increased its publication rate in refereed journals.

The School of Business Summer Initiative

As a result of grantsmanship activities, the School of Business has been able to provide educational training to diverse groups--secondary school students, high-achieving business majors and Army civilian personnel. Robert Askew, assistant professor of accounting and finance, has offered junior and senior business majors preparatory training for graduate school as a result of grants received from the U.S. Department of Education. Participants in the program were high-achieving students majoring in business from Hampton and other universities. During the summer, students participating in the program were exposed to modules of courses they would be expected to study in graduate school. One of the major objectives of the preparatory program was to encourage participants to pursue graduate study. Program evaluation indicated that the objectives of the program were attained.

Establishing A Reputation in Executive Training

In 1991, the School of Business received a grant from the Department of the Army to provide mid-career advancement training for civilian employees of the Army. Dr. David Beaty, director of the program, reported that the average age of those who participated in the 1991 summer session was 42, that they all held positions at executive rank, and that they were selected world-wide by the Army for professional development training in the School of Business at Hampton University. Beaty stated that since the program is a premier management training program for the Department of Army Civilian Personnel Managers, "Hampton University can be particularly pleased that the foundation has been laid for obtaining future grants and funding in executive training and development." The university received a second training grant from the Army in 1992.

Junior Achievers Trained at Hampton

Dr. Alphonse Carter, dean of the School of Business, developed a cooperative agreement with the National Urban League's Junior

Achievement Program to train youngsters during the summer of 1992. The program, involving 150 black high school students from Milwaukee, Wisconsin, Pittsburgh, Pennsylvania, and Washington, D.C. was designed to give these future business leaders hands-on experience in organizing and operating a company. In addition, students were exposed to mentors and corporate leaders. Carter felt that the program offered an opportunity for faculty in the school "to reach back into high schools and motivate black high schoolers to more seriously consider pursuing a bachelor's degree and beyond."

School of Education
National Prominence as a Result of Grantsmanship

The faculty in the School of Education were the first group at Hampton University to gain national prominence in grantsmanship. This leadership began in 1969 when Hampton Institute was the only historically black college to be awarded a national Follow Through Model. Funding for some features of the model continued through 1988 under the leadership of Dr. Mary T. Christian, dean of the School of Education from 1980 to 1988. Hampton University's involvement with Follow Through and its Laboratory School provided the impetus for new grantsmanship initiatives in the eighties.

Building on its tradition, the Hampton University Laboratory School became a national mainstreaming model as the result of a funded grant based on a proposal written by Dr. James Victor, professor of special education. The mainstreaming program gave special education teachers training in integrating pre-school handicapped students into the regular classroom.

In 1983, Victor also received federal funds for the organization of a Children's Diagnostic Center. He described the center "as a training site for both graduates and undergraduates and led to the development of a new undergraduate sequence to train teachers of learning and behavior disordered children."

In-Service Programs in Science Education

In the age of technology, it is imperative that teachers gain new knowledge and efficiency in teaching mathematics and science. Through aggressive grantsmanship activities on the part of Dr. Dianne Robinson, director of the Interdisciplinary Science Center, the university received grants ranging from $40,000 to $600,000 for in-service programs in science education during 1985.

In 1986, Robinson received a $600,000 grant from the National Science Foundation. *This grant was one of nine in the nation funded as a model for middle school science education.* The momentum of the initial grants led to the establishment of an Interdisciplinary Science Center linking the Schools of Education and Pure and Applied Sciences in a partnership for the improvement of teaching and learning in the sciences.

Responding to a National Crisis

Under the leadership of Dr. Robinson, additional grant funds served as leverage for the establishment of a major in middle school science. In addition, there was an effort to respond to the national crisis based on statistics showing consistently low performance of American children in the sciences. A number of sponsored outreach programs were offered by the Interdisciplinary Center:

- A summer resident Young Scholars Program for seventh-grade students
- Pre-College Science Enrichment Program for secondary school juniors
- In-service science education programs for elementary-, middle- and secondary-school teachers
- Scientific tours of wetlands and other natural phenomena for middle school teachers of the Hampton Roads area.

Increasing Minority Success in Grantsmanship

Even with the apparent success that Hampton faculty enjoyed in securing funded grants in the eighties and early nineties, there continues to be significant differences between the success of black proposal writers at historically black colleges and universities and the success of proposal writers--blacks and whites--at predominantly white colleges and universities of comparable size and mission. Many factors contribute to these disimilar results, not the least of which is the support system for grantsmanship and research at each university.

In the fall of 1991, Dr. Reginald Jones, chair of the department of psychology and a prolific writer, sought to make a difference by establishing a National Center for Minority Special Education Research and Outreach. The center was developed with Dr. James Victor, associate director for Minority Special Education Research and Outreach, and was funded for four years at $900,000 per year. Its goal was to provide technical assistance to HBCU's and other institutions of higher education having twenty-five percent or greater minority enrollment, in the preparation of grant proposals for research and demonstration projects in special education, rehabilitation and related fields.

Faculty Development in the Humanities

One of the major components of the general education program begun in the fall of 1991 was the interdisciplinary humanities course. Prior to the establishment of this course, it was necessary for faculty to engage in a series of professional development and curriculum development activities. Dr. Enid Housty, director of the humanities core, was the major force behind the restructured humanities course. She received funding from the National Endowment for the Humanities to enhance the teaching of Humanities 201-202, which enabled the faculty to study oral epic traditions in Africa, Greece, Rome and Medieval France in seminars conducted by such scholars as Daniel P. Kuene, professor of African languages and literature, University of Wisconsin-Madison; Jon D. Mikalson, chairman, department of classics, University of Virginia, and Edward A. Heinemann, professor of Medieval French literature, University of Toronto. As a result of the seminars, teams of faculty members in art, music, literature and history restructured the humanities course to integrate conceptual information about Western and non-Western cultures.

School of Nursing Serving Those Least Served

During the 1980-1991 period, the School of Nursing was the flagship school in pursuing grants. Dean Elnora Daniel and the school faculty were highly successful in procuring external funds which involved new program initiatives, student financial support, outreach activities, and international development. Among those grants of far-reaching impact was the $746,000 received by the school in 1985 from the W.K. Kellogg Foundation.

According to Dr. Daniel, "The award was used to implement an interdisciplinary nurse-managed health center with a mobile unit that provides health care services to medically unserved and underserved residents of communities in Hampton, Newport News, and York County, Virginia. Clients of all ages benefit from health screening and risk appraisals, education and counseling. Particular emphasis is placed on the health promotion needs of adolescent and geriatric populations." Further, Daniel pointed out, "The Nursing Center serves as a site for faculty practice, consultation, clinical research, and provides non-traditional learning experiences for both undergraduate and graduate students. The 'Health Mobile' provides health care services at area churches, shopping centers and community centers in Hampton, Newport News, and York County."

Continuing Education for Practical Nurses

The School of Nursing, while having both a bachelor's and master's degree program, was able to play a role in upgrading the education of practical nurses through its proposal-writing activities. In January of 1984, a continuing education program was instituted as the result of a grant from the Teagle Foundation for approximately $400,000. The purpose of this three-year project was to expand continuing education activities and offerings available to practicing registered nurses and licensed practical nurses.

Increasing the Pool of Black Nurses

Sponsored programs enabled the School of Nursing to reach still another group of society--that is, black students with educational weaknesses. Beginning in 1983, a $500,000 three-year grant funded under the Women's Educational Equity Act was used to begin Project BEST (Blacks Educated Successfully for Tomorrow) in the School of Nursing. The project involved a support model designed to reinforce the cognitive and communication skills fundamental to nursing education. Summer courses, which focused on basic mathematics, biology, communication skills, and reading, were integral components of this project. During the regular academic year, Project BEST students participated in tutorials designed to meet their learning needs. As a result of Project BEST, a number of students entered the profession who might have been left out.

International Outreach

In 1986, the School of Nursing was also awarded a grant of approximately $100,000 from the Central American Peace Scholarship Program (CAPS) to implement nursing education opportunities for professional and practical nurses from Belize City, Belize, Central America. The faculty offered the international students courses which provided in-depth theoretical components supported by a scheduled clinical rotation encompassing various learning experiences in neonatal and pediatric intensive care units, acute and chronic pediatric care facilities, family planning clinics, labor/delivery, nursery and post-partum units. The selected nurses from Belize were introduced to the American culture and our "way of life" through visitations to various historical and cultural landmarks.

The Center for Teaching Excellence

In a small institution of higher education, it is especially difficult for faculty to meet the triple demands of teaching, research and scholarly pursuits, and significant service. Maintaining a balance among these often conflicting forces is a matter of concern of faculty and administrators at all institutions of higher education. The brief description of a few of the changes that resulted from individual faculty proposal initiatives clearly suggests that faculty at Hampton University took on grantsmanship as a viable part of their professional duties. However, professors are constantly in need of renewal, and one of the most beneficial outcomes of the proposal-writing activities of the eighties was the establishment of the Center for Teaching Excellence.

Upon receipt of a planning grant from the Bush Foundation in 1987, a team of faculty members together with the vice president for academic affairs and school deans wrote a proposal to establish a faculty development unit. The Bush Foundation funded the center for a three-year period in 1988. A second three-year grant was received in the spring of 1991. The Center for Teaching Excellence (CTE) has become the focal point for research, curricular change, instructional improvement, professional collegiality, and the gaining of new knowledge and skills. Internal and external evaluations reveal that, without a doubt, the unit has been the greatest force on the campus in stimulating the growth and development of the faculty. The center is housed in a modern complex within the Science Technology Building.

According to the director of CTE, Dr. Linda Petty, there are several significant factors that serve as a foundation for this effective faculty development center: (1) establishment and maintenance of an active, collaborative partnership with faculty and administration in order to receive the input necessary to plan and operate effectively and efficiently; (2) utilization of faculty with special skills and expertise to help develop and implement CTE activities and projects; (3) maintenance of the CTE as a warm, friendly, supportive place conducive to the free exchange of information, ideas and resources; (4) selection of CTE staff on the basis of their demonstrated dedication and strong commitment to excellence in all areas of their professional lives and their ability to provide significant service to their faculty colleagues. The following is a list of services offered by each CTE program component:

Faculty Development and Evaluation

- Provides information on linkage of course objectives and student outcomes

- Provides expertise on research in college student learning theory
- Conducts seminars on effective teaching strategies
- Supports video-taping and self-critique of class sessions
- Provides information on course outcomes measuring techniques
- Maintains contact with recognized experts on college students and their learning
- Provides faculty with opportunities for upgrading their teaching knowledge and skills directed toward the improvement of student outcomes
- Assists faculty in designing measurable teaching outcomes for their courses
- Facilitates inter- and intra-departmental arrangements for the improvement of teaching and learning strategies
- Assists faculty with experimental design, statistical analysis and writing for publication
- Assists faculty in the conceptualization, preparation and submission of grant proposals

New Faculty Orientation and Development

- Plans and conducts new faculty orientation seminars
- Assists new faculty with development of course syllabi
- Provides mentors for new faculty
- Assists new faculty as they interact with other areas of the university
- Provides new faculty with information that will facilitate their entry and adjustment to the university

Course Planning and Development

- Provides information on innovations in teaching such as guided design and writing across the curriculum

- Assists faculty in the design, development and implementation of new or revised courses aimed at the improvement of student outcomes
- Assists faculty in the design and use of valid and reliable student performance measures
- Assists faculty in the utilization of instructional technology, including computer-based learning systems

Instructional Services and Technology

- Identifies and utilizes information on college student learning styles
- Provides information and expertise on new instructional technologies such as computer assisted instruction and satellite distant learning
- Assists faculty with the construction of reliable tests
- Provides linkage with experts on the new technologies for instruction
- Works with the Teaching Learning Technology Center to provide hands-on experiences with new instructional technologies.

Center Administration and General Services

- Administers mini-sabbatical program
- Serves as a clearinghouse for existing and future projects on student outcomes assessment
- Provides technical consultation in the selection and design of assessment instruments and the interpretation of student outcomes
- Assists faculty with preparation of documentation for tenure and promotion review
- Organizes and interpret student outcomes data for appropriate academic units
- Provides small and large group presentations in the areas of curriculum, faculty and student development

- Maintains a faculty lending library of books, journals, video and audio tapes in all areas of professional development and interest
- Coordinates the overall planning, development and administration of CTE activities
- Consults with faculty on professional problems

Evaluations from both outsiders and Hampton faculty themselves have been uniformly enthusiastic.

Dr. William Brazziel of the University of Connecticut, external evaluator for CTE, pointed out, "The introduction of the center to the Hampton faculty and administrators was outstanding. The effort guaranteed enthusiastic acceptance. . .Faculty members accept the center. . .Most important, they know it is there as a place where they can find an amazing variety of services to help them in their efforts to enhance the Hampton experience for their students."

Bush Foundation evaluator, Georgia State University Professor Asa Hilliard, while visiting CTE indicated that clearly, something important and very effective is happening at CTE. He also said that every faculty member that he talked with raved about the atmosphere and the services available to them at the center. Hilliard believed that the exceptional staff is the critical force behind the effectiveness of the Center for Teaching Excellence.

And Harvard University Professor Dean Whittla, Bush Foundation site visitor, said that he did not want to recommend that CTE put any more activities on its plate. He expressed amazement at the broad range of effective services and activities available, and said that he felt that the center was providing an excellent service.

Faculty Comments

The center is designed to serve the faculty. Here are faculty comments about the effectiveness of the center:

> *"I was able to publish the results of my research in a refereed journal as a direct result of the assistance that I have received from Dr. Petty in the design*

of my study, the data analysis and with the write up of the report."

"I could not survive anymore without CTE. I can always get aid and assistance with any instruction or professional problem there. When I feel down and discouraged, I stop by CTE and the warm, caring people there rejuvenate my spirit."

"As an outgrowth of the aid and assistance that I received at CTE I was able to get a hundred thousand dollars in grants for my department."

"I always learn so much at CTE workshops and have such a good time."

"Excellent help with course development and instructional techniques!"

"A stimulating environment--I can always get excellent advice on teaching, research and my personal development."

"I love the newsletters--Report To The Faculty. I always read them and try to put the helpful, challenging information to use in my classes. Keep up the good work."

"The high point of my week is when I have time to stop by CTE for a cup of coffee and some stimulating conversation with colleagues about teaching and research."

New Faculty Evaluate Services

Upon receipt of the initial Bush Foundation Grant, the usual half-day new faculty orientation program was transferred to the Center for Teaching Excellence. There, it became a year-long program. Annually, Dr. Linda Petty has the faculty evaluate the CTE New Faculty Orientation Program. In 1991, the group expressed its gratitude for the monthly seminars and the counsel received as they encountered and overcame obstacles during their first semester at HU. They felt that the orientation program should not in any way be changed. In response to the question "Have you experienced any benefits from your association with CTE?" faculty members spoke enthusiastically:

> *"Absolutely, particularly in terms of success in the classroom and working with faculty from other departments."*

> *"Yes! Dr. Petty is so helpful and she really cares about other people. She is the greatest asset that the administration has with new faculty."*

> *"The services are great as they are."*

> *"The seminars were just what I needed. Every subject was helpful and the person that made the presentation was the person in charge of the area on campus. Dr. Petty put us in contact with the most helpful and knowledgeable people in every case. I found that I knew more than many people in my department about some things that came up in department meetings."*

> *"Keep up the excellent seminars--they made me feel at home and I have a place where I can come for information and help."*

The Bush Foundation grant continues to make a difference in the quality of the academic life of the faculty.

Summary

Fund raising and development are critical to the lifeline of an institution such as Hampton University. With the direction and leadership of the president and vice president for development, a strategic plan and support system were developed that resulted in the procurement of funds from the private sector, foundations, state and federal agencies. While it is significant to note that grants and gifts amounted to the acquisition of funds beyond those received in any other comparable time-span in the history of Hampton University, the more important assessment is the impact these funds made on the operation of the institution. Money truly made a difference.

As a result of a successful capital campaign, gifts from private donors and aggressive grant proposal writing to private, state and federal agencies, the university was able to achieve the following:

- Provide more scholarships
- Support deserving students with financial needs
- Attract and maintain a cadre of outstanding faculty members
- Establish research centers
- Provide special training and assistance to faculty and external groups
- Enhance teaching and learning within the university
- Implement a general education core
- Provide state-of-the-art instructional equipment and facilities
- Improve and build new facilities
- Change the academic course of the university

During the 1978-1992 era, development activities made possible through the procurement of external funds did indeed play a vital role in the overall growth of the university.

A PERIOD OF PROSPERITY

Hampton's economic growth--evident throughout the campus--was a typical cooperative effort, led by the aggressive fund raising of President William R. Harvey, followed by the strategic planning of the office of development and the strong support of the alumni.

Moreover, credit must be given to the more creative recruitment efforts of the office of admission, the long-range planning facilitated through administrative services, the success of faculty and academic deans in securing external funds, the reputation and diversity of the academic programs, the confidence of external constituents in the university, the commitment of the boards of trustees to the present and future development of Hampton University, and the bullish management of fiscal and physical resources by the business office. All of these people were responsible for Hampton's acquiring significant fiscal resources needed to build new and to improve existing facilities and buildings.

It is especially difficult to manage a corporation like Hampton University on a fiscally sound basis when the economic market is volatile and the federal government is essentially bankrupt. Yet, it was under these circumstances that Hampton managed to demonstrate the greatest financial vitality and stability in its history.

Withdrawal of South African Investment

These were the best of times for Hampton University, but also the worst of times for much of the rest of the world. It was in this period that President Harvey approached the board of trustees to ask that it stop investing university funds in stocks and bonds in companies conducting business in South Africa or with the government of South Africa. Approving this request could be reflected in reduced revenues from investments and from the endowment. It was, however, the position of President Harvey, faculty and students that Hampton University would not be a party to oppression, even for financial gain.

Establishing a New Management Style

Between 1978 and 1991 many new fiscal and physical management practices were introduced. Lucius Wyatt, vice president for business affairs and treasurer, had the greatest responsibility for these management changes. Wyatt had been involved in some aspect of the business and plant management from the time he was a student worker to his becoming a vice president--a period of more than thirty years. He was therefore the most knowledgeable member of the president's cabinet about the history of the university's academic and service facilities, its strengths and weaknesses.

It was a significant move on the part of the new president to elevate Lucius Wyatt to the position of vice president for business affairs and treasurer. In this role, Wyatt managed not only the fiscal affairs of the university, but also the support staff, buildings and grounds, auxiliary services and security. Second to the president, he had the greatest responsibility for the day-to-day operations of the university as well as the management of its fiscal resources.

Physical and Fiscal Transformation

During the period 1978-92, changes in the fiscal management of resources transformed the skyline of the university. The Hampton University fiscal and physical management model developed during the Harvey years can be seen as one of the most successful operations of its kind in a predominantly black institution of higher education.

In his report to the board of trustees, Wyatt presented an overview of those developments. According to the vice president, during this period from 1978 through 1991, actual revenue increased from $18,106,127 as of the fiscal year 1978-79 to $64,977,323 in 1990-91. In 1977-78 current budget operations resulted in a deficit of $421,091. The next year, 1978-79, a surplus of $72,368 was realized from current budget operations. For each year since that time through 1990-91, the university's current budget operations have resulted in a surplus for each fiscal year.

These favorable results are attributed to many factors. First, in 1978-79, an alternative budget of quarterly allocations was approved by the board. This change put a cap on spending during the quarters rather than making the total amount of annual budget available at the beginning of the year. Secondly, the university changed its marketing style. It no longer relied solely on traditional recruiting activities, but began to assertively project a positive image of academic excellence and financial stability. The new Hampton was a fiscally stable business enterprise and an excellent institution of higher education. This new strategy resulted in a substantial increase in enrollment beyond expectations, while annual budgets--in projections of revenue and in expenditures--remained extremely conservative. The university's annual budget was increased from $16,649,882 in 1978-79 to $60,784,150 in 1990-91.

Endowment Growth

During the early part of the 13-year period after 1979, there was also an increase in endowment income attributed to high interest rates and increases in revenue from gifts and grants. This increase assured the university of additional funds to provide not only for an excellent academic program, but also to make major repairs and renovations of facilities suffering from deferred maintenance. As a result, facilities became more adequate and suitable for an expanding academic program.

The endowment fund also showed unparalleled growth during the period. In 1977-78 the value of the endowment, excluding quasi-endowment, was $29,277,705. At the end of the fiscal year 1990-91, the value of the pure endowment fund was $64,781,369 with an additional amount of $12,339,308 in quasi-endowment, bringing the total value of all invested funds to $77,120,677. In addition, the amount of income generated by the endowment increased from $1,693,437 in 1977-78 to $4,121,928 in 1990-91.

The amount of federal grants also increased from $3,805,342 in 1977-78 to $13,135,811 in 1990-91. This increase had a tremendous impact on current financial operations through the reimbursement of indirect costs.

Annual Budget Surplus

Strategic fiscal planning and astute budget management at all levels of the university resulted in Hampton's having a budget surplus for 13 consecutive years.

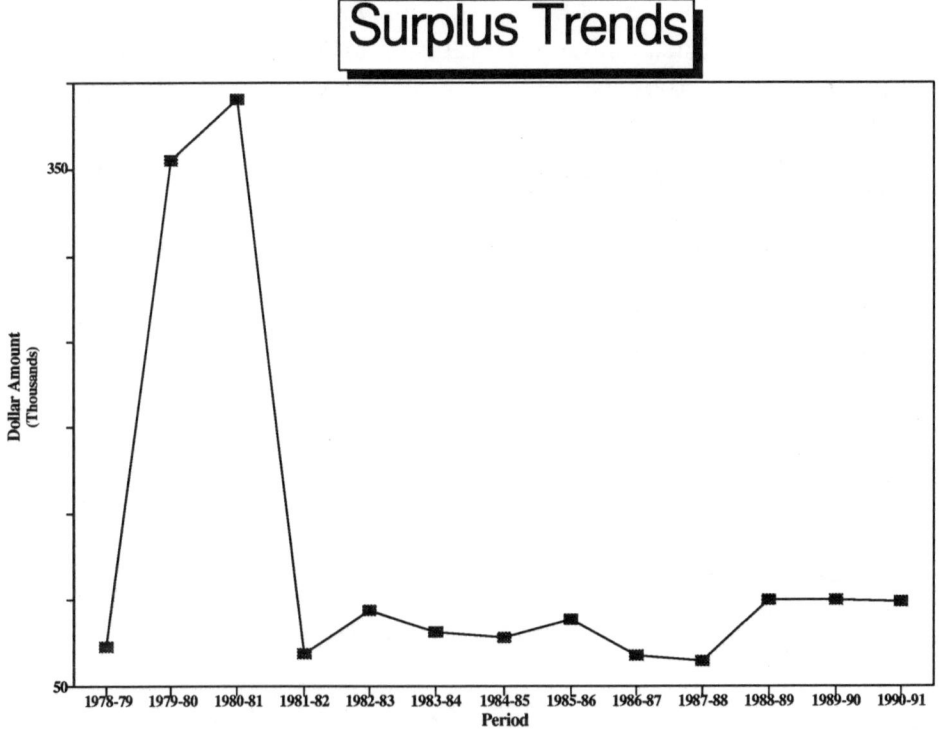

Budget surpluses ranged from $64,513 at the end of the 1987-88 fiscal year to a $390,139 surplus in 1980-81. The entire university has profited, for these annual fiscal surpluses were used to up-grade equipment, provide funds for special conferences, improve buildings and grounds, make needed improvements to campus facilities, provide support to faculty for special projects, and give bonuses to staff and faculty.

By any objective measure, maintaining a surplus in the budget for 13 consecutive years constitutes a phenomenal feat, especially during a period when the country as a whole was in a depressed economic state. Hampton's accomplishment must be attributed to skillful fiscal management. In spite of the two great shocks in the economy--the severe recession of 1981-82 and the October 1987 stock market crash--the administration was able to keep the university on a prosperous course during those periods.

It should also be noted that the general increase in budget allocation reflected the continued demand for additional faculty, state of the art equipment, program expansion, and a host of other needs. The ability to meet these budget demands is a further reflection of the effectiveness of the university's fiscal management system.

Moving with the Flow of the Market

Private universities like Hampton need a steady stream of funds to ensure their future economic viability. Hampton's president therefore had no greater priority than that of increasing the university's endowment--since all other functions grow out of the availability of adequate funds.

In the past, Hampton had been fortunate enough to have the resources needed to counter the rapid growth of inflation and the spiralling costs associated with faculty, services, and support. Normally, the president, the vice president for business affairs and the financial committee of the board of trustees at Hampton closely monitored the activities of the university's investment manager.

But during this period of growth, the university broke the tradition of having its funds managed by one investment management firm. Instead, it sought a more diverse administration by hiring several managers who were urged to seek revenue and growth more aggressively.

During the 13-year period the average annual growth rate of the university's endowment at cost was 6.2%. This rate, however, fluctuated from year to year. For example, during the 1978-79 academic year, the percentage increase at cost was 0.35%. It grew in 1980-81 to a high of 12.01%. However, during the severe recessions of 1981 and 1982, this rate fell to 3.65% and 1.48% respectively. It rose to 17.05% in the 1984-85 academic year and fell again in 1987-88, the year of the "market crash". The table that follows details this pattern of overall growth despite the volatile circumstances.

Years	Endowment at Cost	Cost % of Increase	Endowment at Market	Market % of Increase
1978-79	$34,171,112	.35	$30,948,995	3.47
1979-80	34,750,592	1.70	33,425,013	8.00
1980-81	38,924,152	12.01	37,933,919	13.49
1981-82	40,344,714	3.65	38,417,361	1.27
1982-83	40,943,115	1.48	46,587,850	21,27
1983-84	45,557,095	11.27	44,982,878	(3.45)
1984-85	53,325,782	17.05	59,413,349	32.08
1985-86	58,881,256	10.42	76,653,928	29.02
1986-87	65,614,337	11.44	75,558,996	(1.43)
1987-88	67,385,012	2,70	71,201,499	5.77
1988-89	70,409,555	4.49	77,154,136	8.36
1989-90	71,701,286	1.83	78,353,652	1.55
1990-91	70,086,110	2.25	77,120,677	(1.57)

The value of the endowment at market has shown greater fluctuations than the endowment at cost. The annual average growth rate at market is 9.06 percent. The value of the endowment has followed the fluctuations in stock prices. Between 1984 and 1986, the rate of market increase in the value of the endowment was as high as 32 percent. With the crash of the stock market in 1987, the endowment registered a negative growth of -1.43 percent. And, because of the economic slowdown that began in 1991, the growth rate for the endowment was also negative for the period 1990-91.

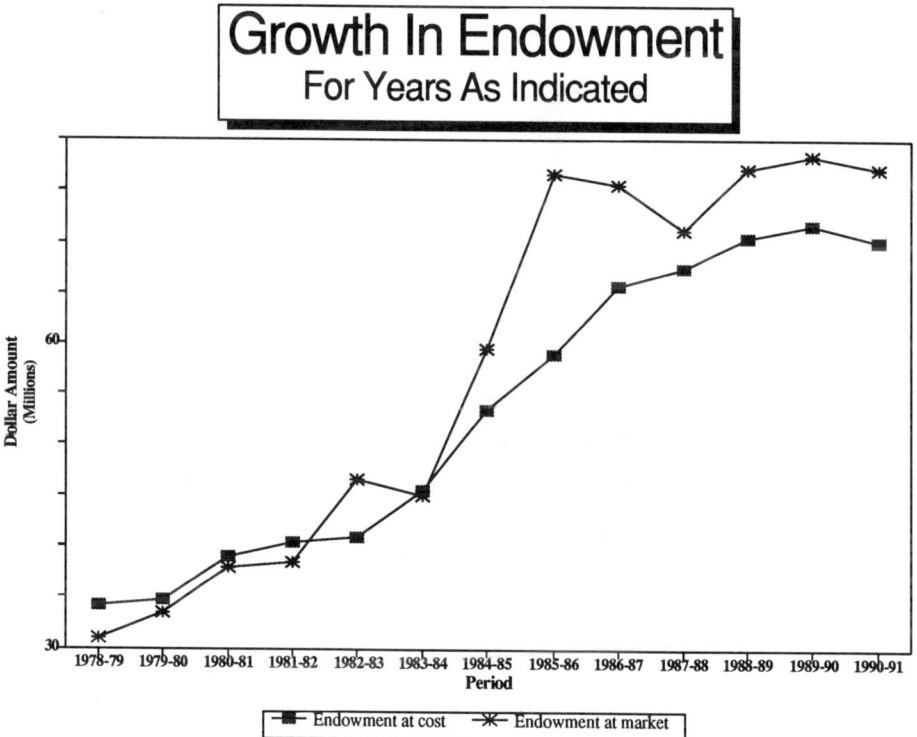

Hampton University Is Big Business

It has become increasingly apparent in the decade of the eighties and into the nineties that the president of any university, and especially one of a private institution, needs budget management skills similar to that of a CEO of a corporation of comparable size and complexity.

During this contemporary period, Hampton's president provided leadership for the adoption of a long-range planning model. One of the critical components of this model is the integration of budget requests with long-range planning. Accordingly, all unit supervisors were required to submit their long-range plans for a five-year period. Once the plans were approved, annual budget requests were reviewed in terms of the long-range plans of the unit. This procedure enabled the university to develop a cohesive financial map which addressed both immediate needs and long-range projections. If the long-range plan had to be revised, the administrator of the unit was expected to submit an amended document for a second review by an analytical studies team.

Close monitoring of both the budget and planning process resulted in consistent growth in the university's budget. Over the 13-year period, the budget increased yearly with the exception of 1983-84, when there was a 0.3 percent budget decrease in comparison with 1982-83.

The size of the yearly budget is an accurate reflection of the fiscal vitality of the university. As one reviews the next two tables, it becomes apparent that more and more resources were used to support a growing university.

A Period of Prosperity 85

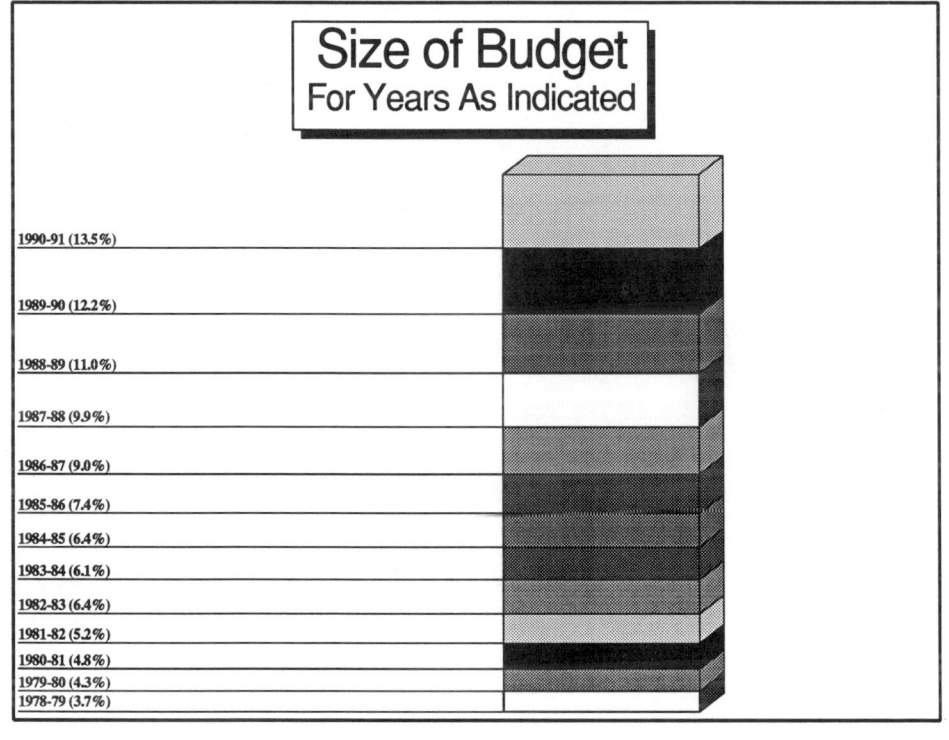

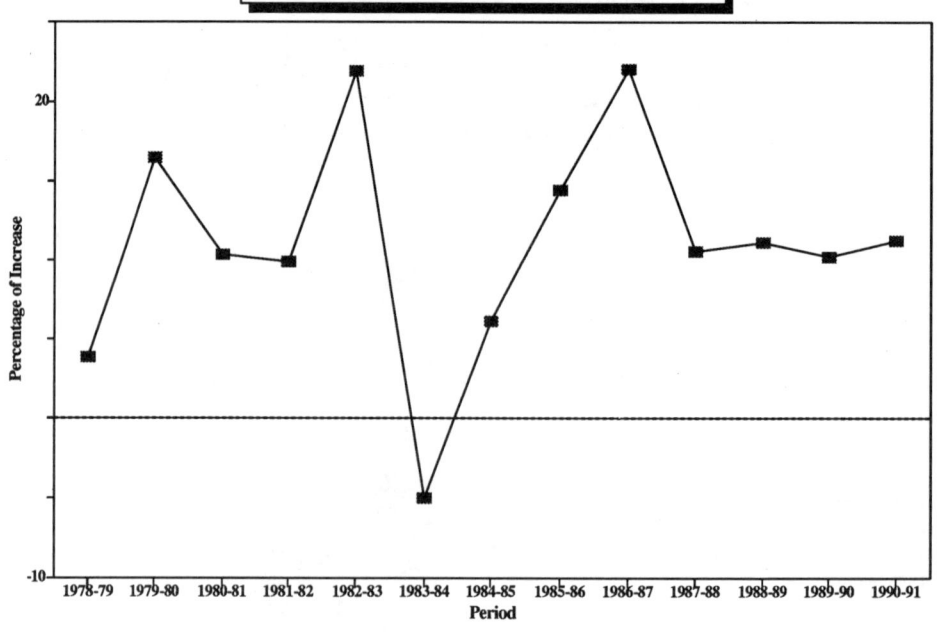

Income and Expenditure

Budget management was carefully monitored by the office of the vice president for business affairs and treasurer. Although budgets were approved at the beginning of the fiscal year, allocations to units were made on a quarterly basis in order to avoid over- spending in needed areas prior to the end of the fiscal year. This policy resulted in all supervisors taking responsibility for avoiding budget overrun. When a unit submitted a request for expenditure that exceeded the quarterly allocation, it was denied. There was a general management directive that "one does not spend what he/she does not have." This policy helped immeasurably in balancing income and expenditures during the 13-year history as indicated below:

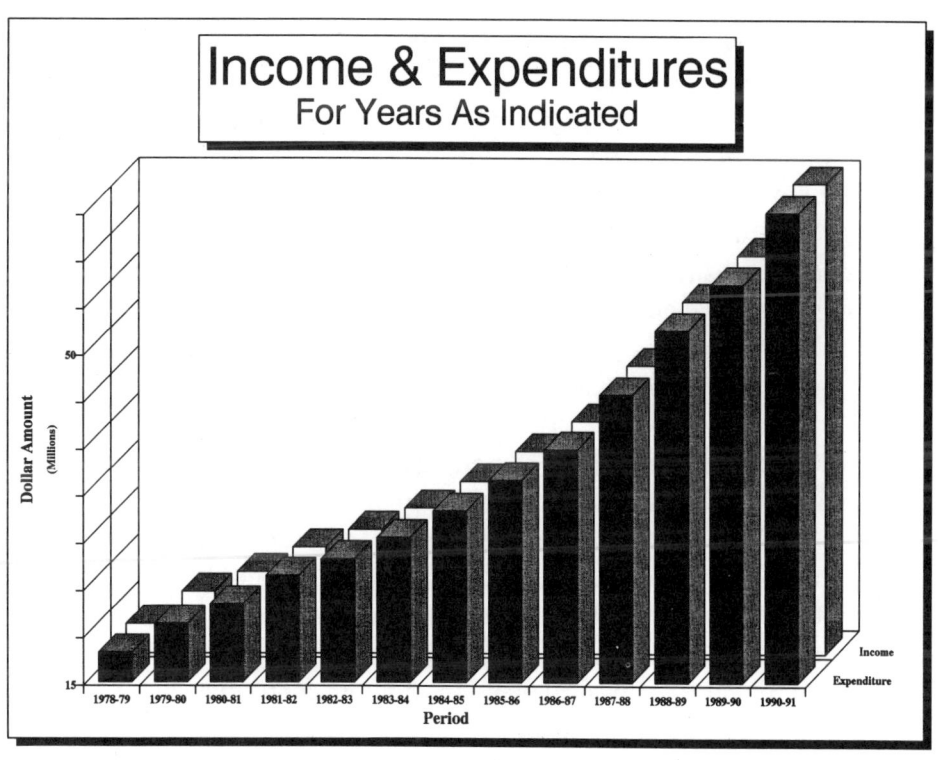

It is not too bold to assert that fiscal management at Hampton University, during a period of national economic decline, was much more responsible than that of the federal government. Sound budget management was indeed a priority for every unit--including academic affairs, auxiliary services, buildings and grounds, student affairs and other support units--and became a model of institutional teamwork.

Visions of the Present

In the historic brochure *Visions of Our Past*, one finds a listing of structures which were completed during the early days of the institution. Included are descriptions of the orange-beige brick structures which were built during the era of Jerome H. Holland. These represented the Centennial Campus and were given that identity because they were constructed during the sixties as part of the celebration of the 100th birthday of the university. Many of these buildings were named and dedicated in the seventies, but there was no new full-scale construction on the grounds of the university until the eighties.

It was in the decade of the eighties and into the nineties that those who visited the campus began to find a new environment which might well be identified as visions of the present.

Entering the grounds today, one finds a graceful wrought iron fence extending from the main gate to the far end of campus. This fence, on the street side of the waterfront campus, was constructed in the eighties and adds protection as well as beauty to the grounds.

Changes in the Physical Environment

President Harvey, at the beginning of his tenure at Hampton University, let it be known that physical upkeep was essential to the vitality of the institution. He contended that a bucket of paint used on a scheduled basis could save thousands of dollars in future replacement cost. Consequently, he established procedures for maintenance and repairs to campus facilities, and even scheduled walking tours with the director of physical plant. In addition, appropriate vice presidents and deans were required to identify facilities that were in need of improvements and repair.

All requests for new facilities were first introduced through the long-range planning process. As the result of strategic planning, the already stately campus was enhanced through a series of new construction projects and major renovations. No facet of the 201-acre complex was overlooked. The list below details major improvements:

*New parking lots were constructed, and old ones were paved or resurfaced.

*Old buildings were revitalized and some were relocated.

*Some structures were gutted and new modern interiors were designed and built.

*Old streets were rerouted as new traffic patterns emerged.

*Female and male residential units were remodeled and new facilities were built.

*State-of-the-art electronics networked the campus.

*The football stadium was expanded and lights for night playing were replaced.

*A regulation modern track facility was established.

*A tennis stadium and additional courts were added.

*A warehouse as well as an equipment facility building were constructed.

*Classroom and student services facilities were constructed.

*Study and research structures were renovated and constructed.

*A statue of Booker T. Washington, the university's most outstanding graduate, was added to the grounds.

During the 1978-1991, period the university spent $35,526,012 for construction of twelve new buildings and other structures. In addition, $14,001,904 was expended for renovations and improvement of 25 buildings and other structures.

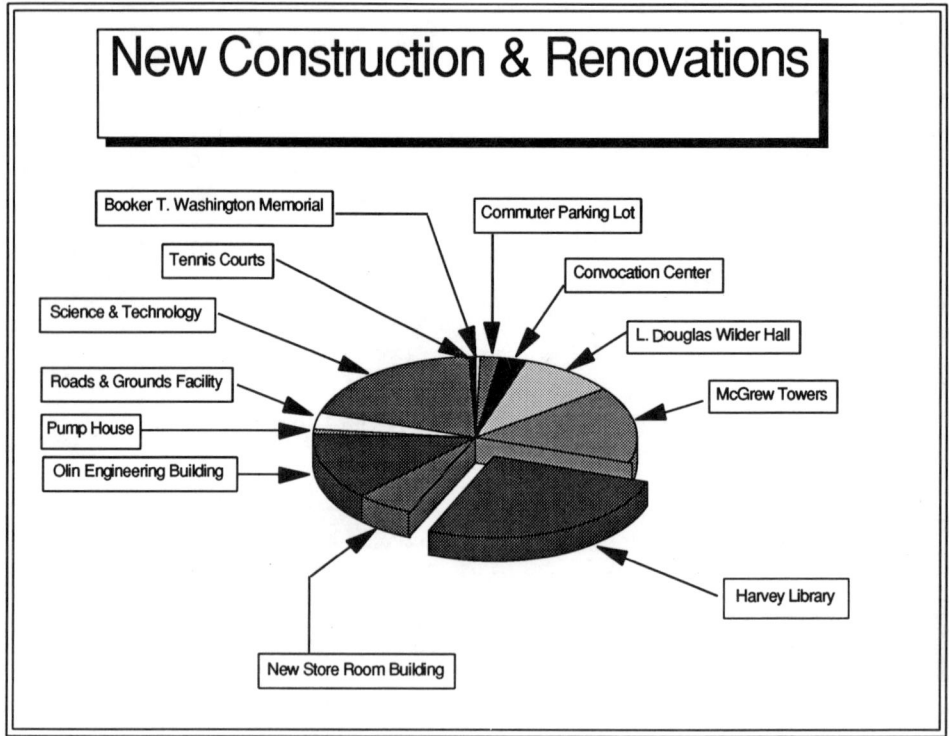

Investment in the Present and Future

In recognition of 13 years of service with distinction, Dr. Wendell P. Holmes, Jr., chairman of the board of trustees, dedicated the new state-of-the-art library to President and Mrs. Harvey at the 1992 Founder's Day Ceremony. The walls of the library are adorned by two murals, *House of the Turtle*, and *Tree House* by the famous artist, John Biggers.

William R. and Norma B. Harvey Library

According to Biggers, "The paintings are a metaphor for the human experience of growing, learning, thinking and developing sensitivity and responsibility." The new library, designed by Hubert Taylor, an alumnus, is capable of housing 600,000 volumes and replaced the outgrown and outdated Collis P. Huntington Memorial Library which could hold 335,000 titles. The five-story atrium facility, featuring state of the art on-line technology, is fully prepared to participate in the information highway of the next century. The outstanding Peabody Collection of African-American History and Affairs is housed in the Peabody Room.

The Livas Design Group, a firm consisting of a number of Hampton alumni, was the architectural firm for this new library and for many other buildings on campus.

Marine Science Center

William Harvey, in his address to the campus and community at his first convocation, said that he wanted the university to offer a major in marine science so that African-American students could be encouraged to enter non-traditional fields. Consequently, the first major construction of the eighties was the renovation of an old cinder block, diesel mechanic instructional building. The Marine Science Building is located at the junction of the Hampton River and Jones Creek, and has the capability for piped sea water intake and drainage.

McGrew Towers

When McGrew Towers Conference Center and Women's Dormitory was completed in 1983, Hattie McGrew was the oldest living alumna of Hampton. This nine-story waterfront structure, based on a cluster concept of four rooms centered around a common lounge and bath facilities, provided needed living space for the increasing enrollment of female students.

The Conference Center, constructed at a cost of $6,500,000, meets the increasing need for the university to offer training institutes, workshops and local, state and national educational conferences. It provides an assembly room, lounge, meeting rooms, office, lobby, and kitchen. This conference center is designed to facilitate a second floor if additional meeting space is required.

L. Douglas Wilder Hall

Students at Hampton University are reminded of the many contributions of African Americans to the United States and the world as they move in and around the grounds. Classroom buildings, residence halls and other facilities are named for those who have made a difference.

So the naming of the new male dormitory after Virginia's first black governor on January 28, 1990, during the month of his inauguration was in keeping with Hampton's tradition. L. Douglas Wilder Hall, a five-floor dormitory built at a cost of $3,421,680 and accommodating 197 male students, faces the Hampton Creek. Its architectural style merges with the historical buildings Virginia Hall and Schurz Hall. These two were both designed by Richard M. Hunt, the architect for the base of the Statue of Liberty, Biltmore Mansion and Yorktown Monument.

Storage Facility Responding to a Need

Universities require a range of facilities to support their operations. In 1990, it became necessary to construct a new grounds facility building for the maintenance and storage of service vehicles and equipment. A two-story, 30,000 square foot storage facility was erected in 1985 for receiving and shipping supplies and also to function as a security storage area.

Adding More Grace and Beauty to Grounds

Entering the campus from downtown Hampton, one immediately senses the beauty of the campus as the wrought iron fence stretches from the lower end of the campus to the main gates through which one enters the center of the campus.

Preparation for the Age of Technology

Both the Science and Technology and Olin Engineering classroom buildings are indicative of increasing demand for professionals with strong backgrounds in the sciences and technical fields. The Science and Technology building serves the departments of speech communication disorders, mathematics, economics, computer science and airway science. The three-story facility also accommodates a modern media services unit, the Teaching Learning Technology Center for faculty as well as an area for faculty development, the Center for Teaching Excellence. The Science and Technology building is a 63,000 square foot, three-story structure, completed in 1986 at a cost of $4,896,744.

Olin Engineering

The Olin building is a symbol of the confidence corporate America has in Hampton University. President Harvey in collaboration with the dean of the School of Pure and Applied Sciences as well as faculty in the departments of engineering and physics, submitted a competitive proposal to the Olin Foundation. As a result of this initiative, the Olin Foundation awarded the university funds to build and equip the Olin Engineering Building. This imposing ultra-modern facility which cost $3,355,906 provides classroom, research and laboratory space for the university's engineering and physics departments.

Football Stadium

Hampton University's growing reputation in sports attracted more individuals to these events. The student enrollment explosion placed additional demands on existing student facilities. In addition, there was increased interest in a diversified sports program. To meet the growing demand, Armstrong field was enlarged and lights were replaced for night games. The track was surfaced and a tennis stadium was erected.

Student Health Services

The university has always had a commitment to providing minimal health services within the confines of the campus. Accordingly, when the old health center became inadequate, an existing building was renovated that provides offices for physicians and more suitable space for other health and medical services.

Whipple Barn
From Barn to Student Administrative Services

In the early years, Whipple Barn was a facility housing horses, cattle and farm equipment. When the university discontinued its agricultural focus the stately barn became a warehouse for supplies and equipment. In the contemporary period such a facility in the heart of the campus needed to be put to better use. So with the combined vision and wisdom of the president, vice president for business affairs and treasurer, vice president for administrative services, director of physical plant and the Livas Design Group, an architectural firm, the old Whipple Barn became the new Administrative Services Center. The newly renovated facility opened in the spring of 1991. Its new occupants include the office of the registrar, the admissions office, the office of financial aid, campus police office, extension of airway science and some units of the business office. The cost for renovation of Whipple Barn was $2,579,223.

William R. and Norma B. Harvey Library

Marine Science Center

McGrew Towers

L. Douglas Wilder Hall

Storage Facility

Football Stadium

Student Health Services

Whipple Barn

Booker T. Washington Memorial

Booker T. Washington Memorial
Recognition of a Famous Alumnus

Booker T. Washington, Hampton's most illustrious graduate, class of 1875, was recognized by his alma mater in March 1984 when his statue was unveiled in an area designated as Memorial Gardens, close to the historic Emancipation Oak. The unveiling of this statue was the realization of a dream held by alumni, faculty, staff and friends of the university.

The Booker T. Washington statue not only stands as a living monument to an illustrious Hamptonian, but it also symbolizes the reputation that the university enjoys in the external community and especially in the Commonwealth of Virginia. Even though Hampton is a private institution, the president, with the assistance of delegate Richard Bagley of the Virginia House of Delegates, received a grant of $75,000 to erect the monument in honor of the university's most famous alumnus. The city of Hampton followed the lead of the General Assembly and named the new bridge leading from Settlers' Landing Road to the campus, the Booker T. Washington Bridge.

Going Beyond The Confines of The Campus

President Harvey's concern for the future economic security of the university led him to approach the board of trustees to establish a separate wholly owned corporation to invest in financial ventures. The board approved the proposal, and one result was the development of Hampton Harbor. The opening of Hampton Harbor was another example of the futuristic approach to resource management at Hampton University. Funds generated from Hampton Harbor are being used primarily for student scholarships.

Summary

The Period of Prosperity depicts a university with:

- A well-managed investment portfolio
- A well-designed short and long-range budget management system
- An excellent record of resource management
- An appreciation for both beauty as well as utility in physical structure
- A sense of priority in providing for instructional and support services for both students and faculty
- Leaders at the helm with well-developed fiscal management skills
- A sense of beauty in the physical environment
- A commitment to survival today as well as in the future

Hampton University enjoyed a period of prosperity in the 1978-1991 era. The 1980's might well be identified as the Decade of Physical and Fiscal Development because there is no other period in the history of the institution in which the endowment grew in spite of a national recession. There is no other period with these features: tremendous renovation and construction, annual budget balances, and a year-to-year surplus.

9

HAMPTON IS FOR STUDENTS

"This traditionally black college will not only survive but will strive. The demand by the selective students who are attracted to Hampton and an excellent faculty will, in turn produce a supply of black professionals who will create a new demand."

Tony Brown's Journal, January 1981

The lifeline of Hampton University is its student body. Every decision, plan and activity is ultimately related to student life. Students represent our national product, and so our primary objective is to serve students. In this chapter, I hope to provide an overview of some of the special initiatives which have been adopted to improve student life at Hampton.

This history cannot include all of the student affairs activities available to Hampton University students. Instead, my focus is on those initiatives which have broad ramifications for the entire campus community. Here then, we shall learn about specially designed recruitment and admission programs including those aimed at students identified as having limited academic promise. Attention will also be focused on the innovative presidential scholarships, our honors residential facilities, the national student leadership program and our athletic victories in regional and national championships.

In no other period in the 124-year history of the university was there a greater demand for the "Hampton Experience." Other historically black institutions were competing mightily for students in the decades of the eighties and into the early nineties. By contrast, Hampton's struggle was with the demands of an ever-increasing population.

New Competition for Minority Students

Beginning in the seventies and continuing into the nineties, recruitment of minority students became a priority among majority institutions. Now for the first time in the history of higher education, black colleges and universities had to compete with white institutions for outstanding black students in both the academic and athletic arenas.

The "creaming off" of top students and faculty by prestigious research institutions through special minority incentive grants, generous financial aid packages and attractive merit scholarships became a challenge for black institutions like Hampton. The president, faculty, alumni and friends of Hampton, while certainly proponents of equal educational opportunities, were also aware of the dichotomy of equal access programs at historically white colleges and universities.

This dichotomy is aptly described by sociologist Robert Staples, who states that many minority Americans "did not become a part of the main fabric of our colleges and universities [white institutions]. Rather they were added to or grafted onto these institutions of higher learning as extras. . . Colleges and universities took credit for enrolling minority students but did not commit themselves to seeing that they graduated. . .Thus, while the front door was open, so was the back door."

In spite of the situation described by Staples, minority enrollment at white institutions continued to increase during the eighties and into the nineties. The new competition for minority students appeared to be a welcome challenge for President Harvey and Hampton's recruiters: the college responded with a carefully designed recruitment program.

Telling The Hampton Story

Dr. Ollie Bowman, dean of admissions, put together a recruitment team that went to key locations throughout the United States to tell the Hampton story through the use of specially designed departmental recruitment bulletins and media presentations. The recruiters focused on academic programs as well as special opportunities for the Hampton student to gain a positive sense of self-worth. In presenting the Hampton story, emphasis was placed on the holistic approach to personal development. Hampton was portrayed as an excellent educational investment, with students who came with high SAT scores and solid secondary school records. Most importantly, Hampton University was shown to have a special ambience not likely to be found among its major competitors. Recruiters and alumni presented evidence that, in addition to accredited academic programs, students at Hampton University lived and learned in a community committed to these advantages:

- Develops and fosters a positive self-image
- Provides countless opportunities for individual leadership development
- Presents successful role models
- Offers opportunities for social interaction with life-long friends, associates and future mates, and provides mentors and support networks

Alumni Recruitment Strategies

Vivian David, director of the National Hampton Alumni Association, Inc., and Alfonso Knight, former director and president, both indicated that recruitment of future Hamptonians was among the top priorities of the association at national, regional and local levels. The strategies used by the alumni involved parents of enrolled students, alumni recruitment committees, pre-alumni clubs, university student recruitment teams, university recruiters and secondary school counselors.

In addition to the combined efforts of these groups, the president himself participated in regional conferences throughout the country, where he gave fireside chats, reporting on the status of the university and responding to questions. These sessions provided alumni with current information on academic programs and other campus developments.

Moreover, these activities were buttressed by the loyalty of Hampton alumni who have always been one of the university's greatest assets. Hamptonians continue to send their children to what they fondly refer to as their "Home by the Sea."

High School Day

The annual High School Day sponsored by the office of admissions brought aspiring Hamptonians and their parents to the campus. A well-coordinated program involving administrators, faculty and students provided an opportunity for high school students to see the campus and have their questions answered. In addition to High School Day, the university's student recruiters conducted daily tours of the university for individuals and groups. These student recruiters were Hampton's best salespersons.

Unprecedented Enrollment

The combined efforts of the office of admissions, alumni, and students, when coupled with the reputation of Hampton University as an outstanding educational institution itself resulted in unprecedented enrollment growth during this period. Requests for special attention from applicants and their supporters came in regularly to the president and other university officials. All of the evidence suggests that college-age black students had great confidence in Hampton University.

According to reports from the office of the registrar, the total enrollment of students at the university rose from 2808 students in 1978 to 5704 students in 1991. Table 7 provides an overview of enrollment growth during that 13-year period. The greatest growth was in undergraduate students. However, with the trend toward older students returning to college, the College of Continuing Education also increased its enrollment when non-traditional degree programs were introduced. And while the enrollment in the undergraduate college remained predominantly black, the enrollment in the College of Continuing Education was in large part white (see Table, p. 103).

Eminent/Presidential Scholars

Hampton truly was going against the odds during this dynamic period. As the recruitment of black students and the availability of lucrative financial aid and scholarship programs at majority institutions became commonplace, many black colleges found it increasingly difficult to attract the best and the brightest freshmen. Not Hampton: it never experienced a decline in enrollment. Still, President Harvey initiated a scholarship program which would honor talented and gifted students who had exemplary SAT scores and secondary school achievement.

The Eminent Presidential Scholars Program was established when the president set aside special funds for students with high SAT scores. Dr. Oscar Prater, vice president for administrative services, established the criteria for these scholarships and administered the program. As more and more outstanding students sought admission, increased scholarship funds were made available. Even with increases in allocated funds, there was never enough money to give to all who met the criteria. The Presidential Scholarships are given on the basis of SAT scores:

SAT SCORES	AWARDS
1000-1090	$1,800
1100-1190	$2,000
1200-1290	Full Tuition
1300 and above	Full Tuition, Room and Board

HAMPTON UNIVERSITY ENROLLMENT
FALL 1978-FALL 1991

	1978	1979	1980	1981	1982	1983	1984	1985	1986	1987	1988	1989	1990	1991
NEW UNDERGRADUATES														
Freshmen	680	849	801	937	914	993	981	950	1177	1360	1423	1181	1398	1199
Transfers	168	174	135	133	146	123	126	151	143	110	88	110	58	75
Special	50	37	43	52	119	125	12	12	9	19	10	4	4	5
TOTAL	898	1060	979	1122	1179	1241	1119	1113	1329	1489	1521	1295	1456	1279
CONTINUING UNDERGRADUATES														
Freshmen	286	220	441	325	382	302	269	272	296	379	388	363	574	506
Sophomores	498	646	674	672	824	851	845	840	898	1053	1239	1301	1033	1078
Juniors	459	471	544	533	587	734	697	703	658	706	812	1016	946	889
Seniors	433	452	423	485	534	564	675	678	772	718	697	867	867	1021
Special	14	10	9	98	13	22	12	7	4	10	-	3	17	9
Unclassified	-	86	-	-	-	-	-	-	-	-	-	-	-	-
TOTAL	1690	1885	2091	2113	2340	2473	2498	2500	2628	2866	3136	3550	3437	3503
GRADUATE STUDENTS	220	224	160	201	305	349	396	356	353	377	403	366	335	361
COLLEGE OF CONTINUING ED.	N/A	N/A	N/A	N/A	N/A	N/A	247	171	172	415	245	131	240	641
GRAND TOTAL	2808	3169	3230	3436	3824	4063	4260	4140	4482	5147	5305	5342	5468	5704

The amount received in the freshman year is guaranteed for a maximum of eight semesters if the appropriate grade point average is maintained. Dr. Harold Wade, executive vice president, assumed the responsibility for administering the program in 1991, and he reports that not only did the university continue to attract an increasing number of outstanding students, but also the number of students who retained their scholarships as they moved to upper-class status also increased.

Establishment of the Honors College

Bringing in bright students was not enough. Considerable study was given to the establishment of a university-wide honors program. A faculty committee, Task Force VI: Academic Restructuring for the 21st Century, conducted an extensive investigation before recommending a three-part honors program consisting of a college-wide honors program, a scholar's residential hall and an honor code for those residing in the residence hall or college.

According to Eleanor Lynch, a member of the task force and first director of the Honors College, the proposal as of 1992 is still being expanded and refined. She reported that the Honors College is in the embryonic stage of development, and with increased involvement on the part of academic departments, there are plans for a comprehensive honors curriculum in selected disciplines.

Honors Dormitories

In 1986, with the purchase of a building adjacent to the campus, the president designated Queen Street Dormitory as the first honors dormitory. Residents receive reduction in housing fees and enjoy special programs for them as well as for the incoming presidential scholars. The office of the director, who plans programs and serves as special advisor to the students, is located in one of the honors dormitories.

Bridging the Gap Between Secondary School and College

Hampton, while recognizing the best and the brightest, began its history with the commitment to serve those least served by society. Through the years, the university has continued to allocate a percentage of openings in the freshman class to those who fail to meet the full criteria for first time admission.

It has traditionally offered this group a special summer pre-college program, Summer Bridge. Potential freshmen enroll in six hours of college courses. A professional staff provides special support programs. At the end of the five-week session, Bridge students' records are reviewed by the dean of admissions and, if they have demonstrated potential to do college work, they are granted admission to the incoming class. The Summer Bridge Program has had a long tradition at Hampton and has enjoyed notable success in bridging the gap between high school and college entrance.

Addressing the Black Male Crisis

Hampton's success with its Summer Bridge provided the confidence and background to design an innovative program for high-risk black male students. The president had become extremely concerned about statistics reflecting the alarming circumstances of young black men nationally, particularly their low rates of college completion. He believed that Hampton University should contribute to the solution of the problem.

In 1989, Oscar Prater, vice president for administrative services, was asked to design a pilot program to admit a small cadre of black males who did not have the traditional SAT scores for college admission but who received strong recommendations from secondary school teachers and nominations from community leaders. A financial aid package was made available to the group, and a special counselor was assigned to the program. This pilot project for black males, called HOPE, was begun in August 1989.

After the first year, Dr. Harold Wade, executive vice president, reported that of the 22 participants in 1990-91, 14 had achieved a grade point average of 2.00 or above. Two students had averages slightly above 2.50. Of the entire group, there was only one withdrawal and two academic dismissals as a result of deficient grade-point averages.

At the beginning of the 1991-92 academic year, 46 students entered the program. But now the program was funded, and the first 26 students to enroll received university-funded stipends of $1,000 each. Project HOPE has become one point of light in the young black male's struggle for survival.

Who Attends Hampton

Throughout Hampton's history, there has been a conscious effort on the part of the president and board of trustees to have a diverse, multicultural student body. From its early days to the contemporary period, the faculty and student body, predominantly black, continue to be a racial and cultural mosaic. In order to maintain a diverse student body, the institution offers special scholarships for Native American and white students.

Hampton has always attracted the sons and daughters of alumni as well as their relatives and even friends. At the beginning of each academic year, Homecoming, Parents' Weekend and Commencement, it is commonplace to meet former students with their own young adults, nieces, nephews, cousins, and young people from extended families who are current enrollees at the university.

The Hampton University incoming class is diverse, but highly representative of America's black elite. In a study conducted by Prater in 1983, he identified certain characteristics of the incoming freshmen:

- 62% were females; 35% male
- 42% of mothers and 39% of fathers had acquired at least a baccalaureate degree
- 43% indicated parental income of $30,000 or more
- 90% had enrolled in college preparatory programs in secondary school
- 70% selected Hampton University in secondary school because of its academic reputation
- For seven out of ten, Hampton was their first choice.

Annual follow-up surveys since the 1983 study have generated similar data.

Hampton University continued to be the choice of an increasing number of students throughout the eighties and into the nineties. In assessing the potential pool of applicants for fall 1992, Dean Ollie Bowman indicated that as of March 1, 1992, the university had received 7,960 applicants for the 800 to 1,000 available slots for freshmen.

The Housing Crunch

The growth in student enrollment had a ripple effect on residential housing, classroom space and student services. In the early to mid-eighties, campus housing became a matter of concern and even some tension among parents and alumni. Alexander Strawn, dean of students, and his staff devised a number of strategies to assign available campus housing. At times, students stood in line most of the night in hopes of getting rooms before all the available spaces were gone. Student personnel staff finally designed a lottery system to relieve some of the pressures. However, the lottery system did not entirely eliminate the anxiety over campus housing.

The president and Lucius Wyatt, vice president for business affairs and treasurer, took steps to increase campus housing space. Personnel in buildings and grounds renovated campus faculty residences, transforming them into student cottages. Funds to build new student residences were secured and off-campus alternatives were found. According to Strawn, the pressure was relieved through what he calls multi-dimensional strategies which included utilization of campus cottages for student residences, purchase of mobile housing units which were then placed in the vicinity of campus cottages, renovation of older residence halls including acquisition of new furniture, and the following measures:

- building of residence halls for both women and men
- installation of telephones in students' rooms in all residence halls
- establishment of honor dorms for both women and men

- construction of apartment units in Hampton Harbor to provide a choice for Hampton students who preferred apartment-type living, but could not afford transportation for other off-campus housing.

Auxiliary Services

With the expanding student enrollment, it became necessary to change the traditional operation of student auxiliary services. The university had long been known for having its own dining service staff to operate its eating facilities. However, maintaining central dining facilities for the increased numbers of students became too much for the in-house staff to handle, and after considerable study, the university moved to bring in an outside contractor to provide food services. According to Rufus Easter, director of auxiliary services, even with the change-over, there was a need for close monitoring. In order to serve students better, an advisory council was formed, consisting of representatives from student government, student affairs personnel, auxiliary services and the food contractor. The council monitored the services and received comments from students.

Increased enrollment taxed another service unit--the university bookstore. The solution was a new facility to meet the needs, and funds were allocated for the movement of the bookstore into a renovated area of an older campus building--Armstrong-Slater Hall. The new two-story facility provided separate floors for textbooks and general merchandise.

Student services were challenged also. While the growth in enrollment was welcome, there was concomitant pressure to maintain services which enhanced student life. Even those units of the university which are seldom recognized as having an impact on students had to be expanded or changed. An example is the transfer of university health services from a cottage to a modern facility with an expanded staff to handle the health needs of the campus community.

Leveling the Playing Fields

Athletics continued to be an integral part of student life. At Hampton University, like most American institutions of higher education, sports often unify students, faculty, administrators, alumni, town and gown. This broad constituency is consistently interested in the athletic records and personalities and feel an undeniable sense of pride in the school's athletic program.

Throughout the eighties, Hampton University's sports programs gained recognition in the Central Intercollegiate Athletic Association (CIAA), the National Association of Intercollegiate Athletics (NAIA) and Division II of the National Collegiate Athletics Association (NCAA). Individual athletes and teams established impressive records and won numerous championships.

Much to Cheer About

Student life involves both athletics and academics. There has always been an attempt to keep sports in balance. This balance has meant that, while winning has its rewards, there has been no pressure to win at any cost. The campus community has much to be proud of. Highlights follow:

--Two Hampton University sports teams have won the NCAA national championships: Women's Basketball, 1988--James Sweat, coach; and Men's Tennis, 1989--Robert Screen, coach.

--Two Hampton University football players have been recruited for professional football since 1978: Don Rose, Kansas City Chiefs and Carl Painter, Detroit Lions.

--One basketball player made the pros since 1978--Rick Mahorn, Detroit Pistons.

--The men's basketball team won CIAA championships in the 1981-82, 1982-83 and 1990-91 seasons.

--The women's basketball team won CIAA championships in 1985 and 1987.

Hit With a Technical Foul

During an exciting athletic competition, one occasionally finds a winning coach or star player being penalized or even ejected for creatively bending or even breaking the rules. When this happens, it causes concern among spectators, media, alumni, faculty and significant others. In 1989, Hampton University found itself in the untenable position of having an external review of the manner in which grades had been awarded to some football players. The questionable manner in which alleged grade changes had been made on some records was indeed a source of great concern among administrators and faculty.

Once it became clear that football personnel had been lax in following established policies, President Harvey imposed sanctions on the program prior to receiving the final report from the NCAA, which required the team to forfeit all the games won during the 1985-86 football season and return the 1985 CIAA Championship Trophy. The team was also placed on probation for two years. While no individual was proved guilty of wrongdoing, the NCAA sanctioned the university's football program for failing to follow established internal procedures.

The episode produced the kind of shock waves that usually follow the referee's giving the coach a technical foul or ejecting a star player from the game. While the controversy over the records of a small number of players was one that the university community would rather not have had to endure, the incident did lead to tightening loopholes in the procedure for awarding credit through examination. The scholarship standards committee changed the existing system by establishment of a pass/fail option rather than assigning grades.

The Boosters

Among the loyal supporters of the university's sports program is a community group composed of alumni and friends of the university who provide moral and financial support. A special section of the football stadium has been reserved for them. In addition to support of home games, the Boosters sponsored tours to out-of-state sites throughout the football season. These activities helped to develop community spirit among alumni, faculty, and community supporters. Administrators, faculty, students, alumni and friends sustained continual pride in the Hampton University Pirates during the eighties and into the nineties.

Student Leadership--a National Model

The development of a cadre of students to serve the university was initiated in 1976 when 50 students who were to hold office in various clubs and organizations were selected to participate in the first student leadership retreat. According to Greer D. Wilson, former director of student activities and student union (1978-1988), "it was clear at the time that the students in leadership positions--presidents of various student organizations and the student government association--required additional skills in order to perform their various roles. They needed an opportunity to interact with one another, learn leadership skills, and discover how to perform their new duties efficiently. The first leaders were selected by the director, and the first retreat was held in the student union, with borrowed mattresses from storage and food prepared in the college grill."

In 1978 when William Harvey was appointed president, the leadership program was expanded and became nationally recognized. Wilson assumed leadership positions in the American Association of College Unions International, which brought other students and college union officers to Hampton for workshops and conferences. Wilson describes the growth and development of the program in a special report:

THE HAMPTON UNIVERSITY STUDENT LEADERSHIP PROGRAM 1978-1988

By 1978 the leadership program had grown to 150 participants. The writer looked for new ways to accomplish the various tasks involved in monitoring the program, while at the same time allowing the students to have the opportunity to practice their leadership skills. The task of selecting new student leaders each year was given to the student leaders. They were taught how to design an application blank, a reference form, and how to conduct interviews. They were then empowered with the responsibility of carrying out the entire process of selecting new student leaders. This process was conducted in the spring of each academic year.

Criteria for Selection

To be selected as a Hampton student leader, the individual must be enrolled as a sophomore, junior or senior student; have earned a minimum grade point average (GPA) of 2.50 on the 4.00 system; be free of academic or social probation, and have secured three reference letters from members of the faculty, staff or administration.

Behavioral Contract, Commitment and Bonding

A behavioral contract was used to ensure that participants understood what was expected of them and what the consequences of breach of contract would be. Problems associated with violations of their contracts were handled by the co-facilitator of the program. Overall, student leaders were highly respected for their contributions by the Hampton students, faculty and staff.

All leaders had to attend a pre-determined number of campus cultural programs and activities. Each student leader purchased a T-shirt that had the theme for the year on it, wore a leadership button, and provided written excuses whenever they were unable to attend an event. Participation in all student leader activities was mandatory. A secret pal program was created for the leaders in an effort to maintain a closeness. Holiday parties, end-of-the-year banquets, and other social events were also incorporated in the program.

Off-Campus Retreats

Each year, the program began with a three-day retreat held at various sites throughout the local area, including the following:

- McKemie Woods Retreat Center, Barhamsville, Virginia

- Camp Young, Norfolk, Virginia
- Virginia Wesleyan University
- Virginia United Methodist Assembly Retreat Center, Blackstone, Virginia
- Wakefield 4-H Center, Wakefield, Virginia.

Among the retreat activities was a love feast held on the second night of the fall retreat. This activity stimulated the creation and performance of original music that was sung at every meeting. Several original songs were composed, such as "We Are Friends," and "Walk Tall Student Leaders." Other songs often sung included "You Have A Friend In Me," "Lean On Me," and "We Are The Bridge." Each leader was required to know the Hampton University Alma Mater, "Lift Ev'ry Voice and Sing" (The Negro National Anthem), the names and locations of the university's administrators, department chairpersons and other information about the school.

After the three-day retreat, student leaders met monthly to discuss issues, receive assignments, and learn additional skills. These meetings were always held in the Williams Student Center.

Faculty as Facilitators

In an effort to maintain the small group experience, faculty and administrators from throughout the campus were selected and trained to work with the students as facilitators. These facilitators were primarily responsible for conducting the training during the three-day retreat. Many faculty and staff worked with their groups throughout the school year. The program, its activities and implementation, were still completed and managed by the director of student activities. Because facilitators were faculty or staff members of Hampton University, an important relationship was established between the director of Student Union and Student Activities, the student leaders, and faculty on the one hand, and with me on the other. This was, as seen by the director, one way to connect the program to various academic departments and also a way to provide students with additional opportunities to interact with faculty, staff and administrators from various disciplines and programs across the university.

Training and Development

Groups of eight to 10 students worked with a facilitator and facilitator throughout the academic year. The workshops were signed by the director of Student Union and Student Activities ; her assistants. Workshops, seminars and programs provided the : dent leaders with skills, information and knowledge in the follow areas:

>Death and Dying
>Business Etiquette
>Personal Finances
>Creativity
>Counseling Skills for Helping Relationships
>Interpersonal Skills
>Committee Management
>Time Management
>Leadership Skills
>Parliamentary Procedure
>Risk Taking
>Risk Management
>Conflict Resolution
>Presentation Skills
>Communication Skills (verbal and non-verbal)

Mid-Year On-Campus Retreat

A second retreat was held on campus every January, with stu(facilitators serving as group leaders. Again, all sessions used the s1 group experiential approach to group dynamics and leadership velopment.

Students Assume Additional Roles

Beginning in 1980, students who had demonstrated a com ment to the program and had excellent leadership skills were sele as co-facilitators. These students were paired with one of the fac or staff facilitators, and the concept of team facilitating evolved. Student co-facilitators were given additional training and responsibilities. Some of these responsibilities included meeting with their group of leaders at least once every month, monitoring the academic progress of their leaders, assigning duties and responsibilities to the leaders, and maintaining information and records. In addition, co-facilitators were responsible for planning, implementing, and evaluating at least one of the monthly seminars and workshops.

Leaders Helping Leaders

Individuals who held leadership positions at the university as well as others who could bring special expertise to the program were recruited to serve as facilitators. As the program progressed, graduates often returned to serve as co-facilitators. The program developed to the point where facilitators, students and graduates of the program all fine-tuned their leadership skills.

Through the years the following persons have served as facilitators:

> **Mr. Darryl Atkinson**, former student leader, department store manager in Atlanta, Georgia
> **Dr. Joyce Berry**, licensed professional counselor, Washington, D.C.
> **Ms. Barbara Chapman**, former graduate assistant, presently counselor, U.S. Army
> **Dr. Sulayman Clark**, former special assistant to the President of Hampton University, now Kellogg Fellow and assistant director of the office of development, Hampton University
> **Capt. Julia Cleckley**, Army ROTC
> **Mr. Ishmail Conway**, former student leader, former director of leadership at Virginia Commonwealth University; presently director of student activities, Cornell University
> **Ms. Carrie Cotter**, former graduate assistant, presently employed at State Farm Insurance Company, Chicago

Ms. Woodrena Curtis, former secretary in the office of student activities, presently training counselor, Fort Monroe, Virginia

Lt. Paul Davis, former Navy ROTC instructor, presently computer specialist, General Electric, Reston, Virginia

Mr. Novelle Dickenson, faculty member of political science department, Hampton University

Capt. Leonard Duncanson, Army ROTC

Mr. Errol Duplessis, faculty member, physical education department at Hampton University

Mr. Frederick Fears, chief accountant, Hampton University

Dr. Lois Fears, former faculty member, Hampton University, department of early childhood education, presently employed at Fort Monroe, Virginia

Dr. Gerald Foster, former dean of the School of Arts and Letters at Hampton University, presently vice president of academic affairs, Virginia Union University

Dr. Reginald Gougis, former faculty member, department of psychology, Hampton University

Rev. Leon B. Hall, former counselor at Hampton University, presently pastor, AME Church in Chesapeake, Virginia

Dr. Carolyn Hines, former director of counseling at Thomas Nelson Community College; presently CEO of C&W Associates

Mr. Woodson Hopewell, former assistant director of student activities, presently dean of men at Hampton University

Ms. Anita Holley, former graduate assistant, Hampton University

Dr. Johnnie Jones, faculty member, department of biological sciences, Hampton University

Mr. Leonard Jones, former chairman of the Hampton Army ROTC Program; presently director of testing services at Hampton University

Dr. Mamie Locke, former faculty in the political science department, presently assistant dean of the School of Liberal Arts and Education, Hampton University

Ms. Frances Moore, former head nurse, Hampton University
Dr. Roberta Morris, former director of counseling center, Hampton University
Ms. Sonya McKeithan, former graduate student, presently community counselor
Ms. Veta Newsome, former graduate student, presently counselor at Rutgers University
Mr. Ernest Parker, former instructor in the School of Education at Hampton University
Ms. Melba Perkins, former secretary to the director of student activities at Hampton University
Mr. B.J. Roberts, chief of university police at Hampton University
Ms. Cordelia Shands, former student leader, presently analyst for Fort Monroe
Mr. Rodney Sprauve, former student leader and reporter for the *Daily Press*
Lt. Kenneth Sutton, Navy ROTC
Dr. Loretta Sweets, former student leader, now assistant professor of nursing, Rutgers University
Ms. Cheryle Walters, former student leader, presently news reporter, channel 12 television in Richmond, Virginia
Mr. Roger Watson, former assistant director of student activities at Hampton University and presently counselor at Norfolk Public Schools
Ms. Yvonne Whitmore, former instructor, mass media arts, Hampton University
Ms. Julia Williams, former principal of Hampton University's non-graded Laboratory School
Dr. Wesley Wilson, former director of affirmative action at the College of William and Mary, presently CEO of C&W Associates
Ms. Brenda Woods, former leader, nursing supervisor, Durham, North Carolina

Inaugurations

One of the yearly highlights of the program was the student leadership inauguration--a time for solemn, dedicated introspection as well as a joyous celebration for installation officially of the student government president, officers and presidents of all campus organizations. A guest speaker delivers an inspirational keynote address to help motivate the students as they undertake additional leadership responsibilities. Speakers for the occasion have included the following:

> The Honorable Ronald V. Dellums, congressman from California
> Dr. Lerone Bennett, writer and historian
> Mr. Tony Brown, journalist
> Dr. Patricia Russell McCloud, orator
> Dr. Maya Angelou, poet and actress
> Dr. Alvin Pouissant, psychiatrist

The Continuation of the Model

Wilson left Hampton University at the end of the 1988 academic year to assume the presidency of the American Association of College Unions International and director of Newcombe Center, University of Virginia. She would doubtless be the first to admit that the recognition and honors bestowed upon her in the profession resulted from the leadership and administrative skills she honed while guiding the Hampton University Student Leadership Model.

The Hampton model is fluid. And although there have been administrative changes, student leaders continue to serve Hampton University.

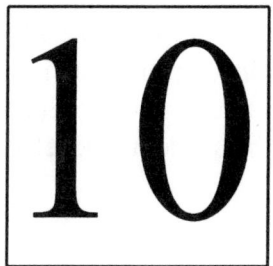

ACADEMICS: HEART OF THE UNIVERSITY

Academics--the heart of any university--are often relegated to a place of minor interest when other institutional matters are considered. And yet, like the heart itself of any body, academics are absolutely critical to the university's well-being.

In earlier chapters I outlined how the university has enjoyed unprecedented success in fund raising, recruitment of outstanding students and management of fiscal and physical resources. However, it should be clear that this attainment has been closely associated with the ongoing development of an innovative academic program and a distinguished faculty.

In his inaugural address, President William R. Harvey set the course that the university would take to reach the academic objectives that he envisioned. One of his first actions to achieve those goals was to create a vice presidency for academic affairs. This administrator was to transform the faculty and academic administrators from a parochial vision of academics to one that was global in perspective, involving not only teaching, but also research and scholarly productivity.

So at the beginning of the 1979-80 academic year, I accepted the appointment as Hampton University's first vice president for academic affairs, and I remained in this post until July 1991. This chapter chronicles some of the academic developments occurring during that 12-year period.

A Year of Innovation

Each fall we selected a theme to establish the special focus of all academic units for that year. The themes centered around contemporary issues in higher education as well as areas in which there existed a need for study and professional development.

Once the yearly theme was identified, plans were put into place to involve the academic community at fall and winter faculty institutes, which were held prior to the beginning of each semester. These institutes were organized as professional conferences, involving keynote speakers, break-out meetings and continuing sessions at departmental and school levels throughout the year.

1979-80, A Year of Introspection

The 1979-80 year was one of review and evaluation. At that time the academic units remained under a divisional structure, and we had to make a decision about future directions. The challenge for academic affairs was to find a way to unlock the hidden talent of the faculty so that they and Hampton itself could be more competitive.

How difficult it is to make changes in an institution like Hampton, which has so much pride and so much tradition. Teaching had always been viewed as its *raison d'être,* and to get more faculty to consider it in collaboration with research and other scholarly activities was a challenge. A typical reaction to the move is found in correspondence to me on October 1, 1980, following a workshop on research.

The senior faculty member who was also chair of the department, posed the following questions:

For many years we have been told that Hampton

Institute is a teaching institution and our first priorities were on good effective teaching. Now we seem to be shifting to more of an emphasis on research. This raises several questions that need to be addressed by the Administrator.

1. *How much emphasis should be placed on research?*
2. *What are the college's expectations regarding proposals, grants, research for each department/ area?*
3. *What departments/areas are traditionally research-oriented and can relate to the greater emphasis on research?*
4. *Which departments/areas have been specifically directed to teaching and may have difficulty with the change?*
5. *What is needed "in house" to develop research-oriented programs?*
6. *What is the college's responsibility to develop the base from which such a research-oriented program will grow?*
7. *Can the current faculty develop the programs as proposed?*
8. *Will the college support recruitment of the necessary research faculty?*
9. *Are part-time persons available to fill in when released time is given?*

The comments are typical of those expressed by faculty when there is a perception that the administration is about the business of changing the *status quo*. However, I kept the letter for a particular reason: it served as a reminder that the faculty has to be at the heart of any plan for change, and that professional development activities must begin with administrators. In addition, the correspondence made clear the need to dispel the myth that research and teaching should be rigidly separate activities.

But most of all, the faculty member's letter to me *became a challenge*. If Hampton was to acquire the status of a comprehensive university in the decade of the eighties, it was apparent that fiscal support, professional development and team-building among constituent groups would be critical ingredients of that success.

Establishing an Action Agenda

In the 1980-81 academic year, with special funds from President Harvey, I established a professional development program called SALT (Special Administrative Leadership Training). This program was to become the principal vehicle for moving the college forward to become a comprehensive university. Initially, the SALT Institutes were limited to administrators. However, when it became known that these training workshops were similar in content to many national conferences, the faculty asked that some of the workshops be planned for them. Using the same acronym (but substituting "Academic" for "Administrative") Special Academic Leadership Training Workshops were scheduled for the week after commencement. Still, SALT continued to be a program chiefly for academic administrators.

During the early 1980's, when intensive professional development training was necessary for the university to prepare a cadre of administrators to assume new roles, additional SALT institutes were scheduled throughout the academic year. The most valuable professional experience of the sequence was generated at the three-day off-campus SALT retreats for deans, directors and chairs which took place after commencement. A description follows.

Sampling of the First SALT Series

Topic	Consultant(s)	Date
The College Administrator and the Law	Viola Taliaferro, Esq. Bloomington, Indiana	July 18, 1980
Why Budgeting?	Mr. Eugene W. Johnson Comptroller Hampton University	July 18, 1980

Administrative Leadership in the 1980's	Dr. Gwendolyn Baker
	Chief, Minorities and
	  Women's Program
	National Institute of
	  Education, Washington, D.C.
		Sept. 26-27, 1980

Funding Ideas and Foundations	Dr. Samuel Robinson Executive Director Lincoln Foundation Louisville, Kentucky	
Proposal Writing and Long-Range Funding Plans	Ms. Megan McLaughlin Program Officer New York Community Trust New York, New York	
Finding Time-- The College Administrator and Time Management	Dr. Boyd G. Sceha Associate Dean, School of Education Auburn University Auburn, Alabama	Nov. 21-22, 1980

Running Higher Education: Evaluation of Administrators	Dr. Nebraska Mays
	Associate Vice President
	  for Academic Affairs
	The University of Tennessee
	Knoxville, Tennessee
	
	Dr. Gertrude Simmons
	Vice President, Academic
	  Affairs
	Florida A&M University
	Tallahassee, Florida
		Feb. 27-28, 1981

Building and Refining The Hampton Institute Administrative Management Model	Dr. William R. Harvey President Hampton University Hampton, Virginia Mr. Lucius C. Wyatt Vice President for Fiscal Affairs and Treasurer Hampton University	Apr. 13-14, 1981

Dr. Oscar L. Prater
Vice President for
  Administrative Services
Hampton University

SALT Institutes were held on a regular basis during 1980-81 so that the deans and directors composing the Administrative Leadership Team (ALT) as well as the Council of Academic Chairs (CAC) could become fully aware of critical issues in higher education. Each SALT institute was evaluated and found to be very effective. They continue to address timely topics and bring to the university outstanding educators from throughout the country.

One of the most noteworthy faculty SALT workshops brought to the campus a team of consultants from the Educational Testing Service in Princeton, New Jersey who evaluated course outlines and examinations as a first step in the development of the university's comprehensive outcomes assessment program.

Faculty and Administrators Address Critical Issues in Higher Education

There was increasing national concern over the direction and quality of higher education in the 1980's. Quite properly, then, the themes we chose for study related not only to the future of Hampton University, but also to the future of higher education in general.

Academic year 1981-82 was the year of "Assessment, Refinement and Accountability." Here the university focused on the needs of college students in a changing society. In response to current trends, an internal review was conducted of past as well as current programs at Hampton. Further, we explored the implications of high technology for program refinement.

In 1982-83, the theme "Enhancement of Academic Programs Through Instructional Technology" served to assist Hampton's faculty and staff in the development of an integrated approach to the use of new instructional technology. My office planned and implemented the first university-wide "hands-on" demonstration of microcomputers as a teaching tool. Also, a special two-week summer training session was conducted for administrators. These efforts encouraged the integration of new technology into the teaching, administrative and research processes.

By the academic year 1983-84, it had become apparent that the academic component of the university was entering a new era of research, scholarly productivity and professional development. Increasing numbers of faculty were successful in securing funded grants, designing and implementing effective teaching strategies, conducting research, publishing in refereed journals, writing professional texts, and assuming leadership positions in professional organizations.

During the 1980's, the Hampton faculty moved steadfastly into the mainstream of higher education. In 1984-85, a year-long effort was designed to address the future from a global rather than a parochial perspective. At the faculty institute in the fall, I established 10 task forces under the rubric of "Academic Restructuring for the Twenty-First Century." This theme provided the opportunity for total faculty participation through workshops, research projects, visitation to conferences and other professional development activities. Each task force was headed by a chair and co-chair with ten members from diverse fields. The task forces were charged with the responsibility of submitting a futuristic document with recommendations for new academic directions based upon 12 months of intensive study. The Twenty-First Century Task Forces had these components:

Task Force I	Admission of Undergraduate Students
Task Force II	Accountability for Our Graduates
Task Force III	Retrenchment of Programs and Faculty
Task Force IV	Common Freshman Year
Task Force V	Establishment of a Lower and Upper Division
Task Force VI	Hampton Institute Student Scholars Program
Task Force VII	Graduate Studies and Research
Task Force VIII	High Technology Across the Curriculum
Task Force IX	Writing Across the Curriculum
Task Force X	Hampton Institute--Today and Tomorrow

Changing the Name of the Institution

The Twenty-First Century Task Forces generated considerable professional dialogue in the scholarly community. The study and exchange of ideas served as a renewal process for both junior and senior faculty. And not only did the recommendations that emerged from this process reinforce some current practices, but they also led to significant changes in program offerings, organizational structure and academic procedures.

The deliberations of Task Force X--Hampton Institute: Today and Tomorrow, for example, changed the course of the institution. The task force recommended that Hampton Institute be re-named Hampton University with Hampton Institute being the designation for the undergraduate college; that the Division of Graduate Studies become The Graduate College, and that a College of Continuing Education be established. These recommendations together with those of an alumni group and a committee of the board of trustees, provided critical data which led to the institution's present title: Hampton University.

The Old Establishment Makes Way for the New

The initial charge to the task forces was to complete their studies in one year. However, it became apparent that some task forces would require additional time. And so it took approximately two years before all of the planning for the future was completed. But as a result of this effort, Hampton University developed an academic blueprint for the 21st century. Many of the proposals have been implemented; others have yet to be fine-tuned.

Basic Skills Competency Required

In addition to the Twenty-First Century Task Forces, a Basic Skills Committee was appointed by the president to monitor the proficiency of entering students in three areas. This committee, under the chairmanship of JoAnn W. Haysbert, assistant vice president for academic affairs, recommended that all entering students be assessed in reading, mathematics and English. Now, all Hampton University freshman are tested in these areas, and those found deficient must enroll in special courses.

Assessment/Accountability Model--Still in the Making

Convincing university professors to assume responsibility for student outcomes is a noble goal, but it is definitely one that requires changes in the traditional assumptions about the role of the instructor. Further, the goal requires certain professional re-tooling. Hampton University's assessment and accountability model has been in the making since the 1981-82 academic year when the academic theme was A Year of Assessment, Refinement and Accountability.

During the decade of development that followed, departments have instituted lower- and upper-division assessment programs, senior seminars, senior theses, standardized testing and test-taking seminars. While school and departmental efforts were commendable, we felt that a coordinated university-wide outcomes assessment model was needed if Hampton graduates were to be competitive with other college graduates.

In the fall of 1990, Linda Petty, director of the Center for Teaching Excellence, received a grant from the Bush Foundation for the development of a university-wide outcome assessment model. It can be described as a pyramidal model of curriculum design and assessment that ensures that all course learning objectives proceed from the program objectives of each department which of course develop from the university mission statement.

Assessment then can be made of each level of these objectives, allowing departments to "x-ray" their curricula, and therefore discover areas of strength and weakness. Instructional techniques that are shown to be robust and effective can be adopted, and improved resources can be solicited to shore up weak points. These interventions can be evaluated at succeeding cycles of the assessment process. These appraisal procedures, therefore, allow faculty to take an empirical approach to teaching in higher education, just as a scientist does in the laboratory. By increasing the feedback to the instructor, these processes allow for timely and systematic evaluation of student learning and instruction.

An assessment facilitator is chosen from each department to work with CTE staff to help them develop all of the skills necessary to serve as evaluation experts within the department. By working with groups and individuals, this facilitator is both an example and a model of the process.

John Alewynse, in his position as dean of freshman studies, received a three-year grant from the Fund for the Improvement of Post-Secondary Education that provided stipends for faculty in English, history, speech and mathematics to participate in post-session seminars. These sessions were designed to assist in developing state-of-the-art instruction and assessment methodologies in those subject areas.

Nationally prominent leaders of these seminars included Pulitzer Prize-winning author and educator Donald M. Murray; Thelma C. Spencer, of the Educational Testing Service in Princeton, New Jersey; James C. Applegate, chair of the department of communication at the University of Kentucky and president of the Southern States Communication Association, and Duke University mathematician David Smith.

Assessing outcomes is a continuing process and the full implementation of a multi-dimensional model is currently being addressed.

Reading And Writing: Everybody's Business

During the 1978-1991 period there was a conscious effort to stimulate "cross fertilization" among departments and disciplines as well as to create a sense of collegiality among the various constituent groups of the university. Two special projects helped to accomplish those goals.

Task Force IX--Writing Across The Curriculum--consisted of faculty from each school and 12 disciplines. From 1986 through 1988, it held a series of campus workshops and external retreats that focused on writing assignments in different curriculum areas. The task force developed publications to assist faculty, and its members were available to help individual faculty members. Booklets addressing common writing problems were published and made available to interested faculty.

Another special event launched during this period was the Hampton University Read-In Program, a joint effort of the arts and humanities faculty and the Huntington Memorial Library professional staff. Held for the first time in the spring of 1988--using Booker T. Washington's *Up From Slavery*--the program sought to have every constituency on campus from the president to the buildings and grounds staff become excited about this specific book during the spring semester. All university administrators, faculty, staff and students were encouraged to read the narrative and to participate in the follow-up lectures, discussions and other events.

The Making of a General Education Core Curriculum

President Harvey made these remarks in his charge for restructuring the general education curriculum at the 1978 Opening Convocation:

> *Good teaching has highest priority at Hampton Institute, for we believe our society needs citizens who can lead, who have high personal and moral standards, who are problem-solvers, and who desire to improve the quality of life for their fellow man. We are concerned with providing the best possible environment for learning for the 3,000 students who come to us from diverse backgrounds--both in terms of prior learning experiences and geography.*
>
> *In this connection, it is worthy to note the new academic direction that I proposed at the September 10, 1978 Opening Convocation. First, I said that a core curriculum should be established which would enable every Hampton Institute student to read, write and do basic computations at a certain level. Additionally, a Hampton Institute student ought to have some knowledge and basic understanding of history, literature and the arts, as well as an opportunity to do some thinking about ethics and morals.*

Changing a program that has an impact on the entire university is a difficult, if not impossible, task at any institution of higher education. It was only through a carefully designed strategy that the new general education program finally came into existence in the fall of 1990. The development of Hampton University's general education sequence is by far the most significant accomplishment in the academic component during that period, for as Cheney states:

> It is through the curriculum that college and university faculties establish a design for education. It is through the curriculum that they communicate what it is an educated person should know...Throughout the 1980's there has been growing concern about the fragmented state of curricula. In reports, books and conferences, educators have talked about the need for greater structure and coherence--particularly in the area of college study known as "general education" (Cheney 1989).

Both the 1978 Harvey mandate and the 1989 national attention to the general education core became significant documents as the faculty struggled with the development and implementation of a revitalized general education program. The chronology that follows suggests the comprehensive process that resulted in Hampton's current general education program.

CHRONOLOGY OF DEVELOPMENT AND REVIEW PROCESS

The General Education Program is a university developed program coordinated and directed through the office of the vice president for academic affairs. The change is a result of the university's efforts to provide a common body of knowledge and experiences for students to build upon as they pursue majors in the various disciplines. Faculty, departmental, and school reviews have been an integral part of the general education proposal. A chronology of the development and review process follows:

September 1978	President William R. Harvey in his initial convocation address called for detailed recommendations for a core curriculum.
October 1978	Core curriculum committee was appointed. Edward Kollmann, chair
October 1980	Kollmann submitted revised report to vice president for academic affairs.
1980-81	Basic skills assessment in reading, writing, and computational skills introduced to all incoming freshmen; other recommendations continued in review stage
Summer 1988	Vice president for academic affairs was asked by president to review general education curriculum in relation to university goals for the 1990's and 21st century; student outcome assessment criteria required by state and regional accrediting agencies.
Fall 1988	Vice president for academic affairs appointed two committees with membership from all schools. Each committee was given copies of 1980 core

	curriculum and other documents related to general education. Hazel J. Garrison appointed chair of university orientation committee Eleanor A. Lynch appointed chair of General Education Program Committee Vice president for academic affairs invited each dean to review general education and submit recommendations.
Spring 1989	Vice president and chair of each committee combined reports and developed first draft of general education proposal. Vice president for academic affairs, chairs of committees, and president met with chairs of each school for input relative to draft proposal. Revision made based on input from individuals and school meetings
Summer 1989	Faculty task force developed content for core freshman course. Course submitted to summer faculty for pilot offering in fall
August 1989	Faculty received draft of revised general education document.

Academics: Heart of the University 133

	Faculty asked to review and provide feedback through schools
September - October, 1989	Vice president met with schools and individuals to receive input and feedback. Each dean sent a written statement to vice president for academic affairs with comments on revised general education proposal. Departmental sequences including new general education received by vice president for academic affairs
November 1989	Vice president submitted revised general education proposal to analytical planning committee and instructional committee.
December 1989	University faculty approved University 101 (new freshman orientation course).
February 1990	University faculty approved general education core.
September 1990	New general education core required for entering freshmen
	Dean of freshman studies appointed

HAMPTON UNIVERSITY'S GENERAL EDUCATION CORE
THE GENERAL EDUCATION SEQUENCE

I. Freshman Orientation   3 hrs.

    UNV 101 The Individual and Life

    A one-semester required orientation course designed to improve the quality of the freshman experience for entering students by helping them understand the purpose and value of higher education at Hampton University as well as the larger context in which that education takes place and the multicultural nature of the problems and concerns which it addresses; to develop positive attitudes toward the teaching-learning process; and to acquire coping skills essential for successful college life.

II. Cultures and Civilizations   12 hrs.

    HIS 106 World Civilization   3 hrs.

    A lecture course surveying the period from the French Revolution (1789) to the present.

    One-semester course to be chosen from:

    HIS 105 World Civilization   3 hrs.
                    or
    HIS 107 African American History   3 hrs.

    Humanities 201   3 hrs.

    A one-semester interdisciplinary course that

explores Western and non-Western cultures from pre-history through the sixteenth century.

Humanities 202   3 hrs.

A one-semester interdisciplinary course that continues the study of Western and non-Western cultures from the seventeenth through the twentieth century.

III. Written and Oral Communication   9 hrs.

    English 101-102   6 hrs.
    Speech 103   3 hrs.

IV. Foreign Language Requirement

Included in discipline core in selected departments

    Major Requirement

English Arts	12 hrs.
English Education	12
Technical Writing	12
History	3
History/Social Science Education	6
Music - Jazz Studies	6
Music Performance	6
Speech Communication and Theatre Arts	
Technical Theatre	6
Criticism and Public Address	6
Interpersonal, Small Group and Organization	6
Theory and Performance	6
Political Science	6
Psychology	6

Sociology	12
Finance	6
Accounting	6
Economics	6
Management	6
Marketing	6
Biology (completion of inter. level)	6
Molecular Biology (completion of intermediate level)	6
Chemistry (completion of intermediate level)	6
Communications Disorders	6
Mathematics	6
Physics (completion of intermediate level)	6

V. Concepts of Mathematics   6 hrs.

   (MAT 109-110 or above)

MAT 109 College Mathematics I	3 hrs.
MAT 110 College Mathematics II	3 hrs.

VI. Science and Technology   6-8 hrs.

(BIO 101 and SCI 102; BIO 103 and SCI 104; or above)

BIO 101 Biological Science	3 hrs.
SCI 102 Physical Science	3 hrs.
BIO 103 General Biology	4 hrs.
SCI 104 Intro. to Physical Science	4 hrs.

VII. Social Science   6 hrs.

Options selected from Economics, Ethnic Studies,

Geography, Human Ecology, Military Science, Political Science, Psychology or Sociology.

TOTAL   46-68 hrs.

Development and Implementation of University 101

One of the unique curricular developments of the era was University 101--The Individual and Life. This course is a classic example of team effort on the part of faculty and staff from diverse fields.

University 101 had its origin in President Harvey's early recognition of its need. At the beginning of the 1988-89 academic year, the vice president for academic affairs constituted a special committee, chaired by Hazel Garrison, dean of the graduate college, which developed a broad outline for the course. Two senior faculty members, Eleanor A. Lynch, director of the Honors College, and John Alewynse, associate director of the Center for Teaching Excellence, developed that outline into a course. Alewynse and Lynch had funds at their disposal to award mini summer stipends to faculty members whom they invited to develop special modules for the course. The instructional units included these areas:

      I.   History of Hampton University
     II.   Black American Art
    III.   The Art of Living
    IV.   Social, Legal and Economic Issues--Personal, Domestic and International
     V.   Science and Technology
    VI.   Health Prevention, Health Maintenance and Illness Prevention

A 400-page course pack developed for University 101 and additional texts were required reading.

Each of the six units listed above lasts two weeks. Students attend three presentations in Ogden Hall and participate in three breakout sessions, taught by faculty representing almost every department in the university. Presenters at Ogden have included a wide range of distinguished individuals from both within and outside the university, including President Harvey himself.

University 101, while not always popular with entering freshmen because of the rigorous demands it makes, smooths the transition from secondary school to college. University 101 is also beneficial to faculty who lead the breakout sessions. The experience of teaching freshmen makes them aware of strengths and weaknesses of entering students and helps them develop a sense of commitment to all students, not just those who major in their discipline.

Academics on the Cutting Edge of Higher Education

Hampton University not only maintained its standard of excellence in existing programs during this era, but also moved to introduce innovative programs which thrust the institution into the vanguard of higher education. Deans, directors and others were asked to identify events, innovations and changes which they felt significantly altered the character of the university. Here are responses:

> *In terms of freshman studies, probably the most significant event of my tenure was the institutionalization of the University 101 Program. . .In addition to its immediate impact upon students, University 101, by virtue of the development and structure of the course overall, also reflects the university's early and ongoing development of a comprehensive assessment strategy.*
> --**John Alewynse**, former dean of Freshman Studies--associate professor of English

> *In 1985, Hampton University's library joined the on-line Computer Library Center (OCLC). . . This introduced on-line and shared cataloging with various other types of libraries throughout the nation to our library. . . The stage has been set for future auto-*

mation... Hampton University has built a new state-of-the-art library. Dedicated and opened for service on January 26, 1992, this modern and effervescent facility has already made its presence felt in a dramatic fashion. It has focused the campus community back toward the library as a central and all-important place in the academic arena.
 --**Earl Bean**, library director

In my opinion, the School of Pure and Applied Sciences has succeeded in meeting several important objectives that are related to the institution as a "university model." The school has become more diversified in its curricular offerings; it has established a strong research base in the departments offering graduate training, and it has enlarged many of its programs to include outreach activities with the immediate and broader educational community. Within such a context, the disciplines have had a positive impact on faculty, students and the university as a whole.
 --**Robert Bonner**, dean, School of
 Pure and Applied Sciences

The following centers were organized in the School of Pure and Applied Sciences during the 1979-1992 period:

Center for Marine and Environmental Studies (1979)
Interdisciplinary Science Center (1989)
Center for Nuclear High Energy Physics (1989); a major award of $5 million was received in 1991.
Photonics Center for the Study of Optics and Lasers (1989); a major award of $8 million was announced in Jan. 1992.
Mathematics Center for Computational Studies in Applied Mathematics and related disciplines.

The establishment of the Center for Minority Special Education has brought significant national attention to the university and serves as a model of cross-disciplinary research and program development between the departments of psychology and education.

The center's purpose is to increase the number of minority personnel and institutions conducting research in special education, to serve as a national center for the dissemination of effective practices, and to develop minority professional personnel.

The establishment of the center has placed Hampton University clearly in a major national leadership position in special education. The center's impact on the field of special education is expected to be substantial in influencing the character of research and development for the next decade.

In the summer of 1990, the university merged the School of Education with the School of Arts and Letters to form the School of Liberal Arts and Education. The merger facilitated the state-mandated restructuring of teacher education in 1987-88. The new mandate required all students pursuing teacher education to complete an arts or sciences major. It also required greater collaboration between units in teacher education and academic major programs. Further, the arrangement we call the Holmes Group membership bespoke a commitment on the part of the university to explore new connections and collaborations between professional education and academic units.

--**Carlton Brown**, dean, School of Liberal Arts and Education

The School of Business has managed to keep a steady course in its drive toward excellence. The curriculum has been focused on the decade of the nineties. Even with unprecedented enrollment growth, the

faculty research and grantsmanship productivity has increased.
> **--Alphonse H. Carter**, dean, School of Business

The International Understanding Program was a federally funded program to expand cultural and global perspectives of educators. Approximately 80 teachers and administrators participated in the program, and international scholars served as lecturers and consultants.

The following year, many of the participants went to Africa to extend and reinforce concepts and knowledge of that country...More than 4,000 children participated in the Young Authors Conference directed by Sharon White-Williams for the city school systems of Hampton, Newport News, York County, Williamsburg, and the Hampton University Laboratory School.
> **--Mary T. Christian**, former dean, School of Education (1977-87) and professor emeritus

Hampton University has a strong relationship with a few select graduate and professional schools like Indiana University, Purdue University, Ohio State University, and the University of Delaware. Their graduate school day programs have attracted some of our brightest and highly motivated seniors to accept an invitation to visit their campuses. They typically perform very well in the department interviews and are offered financial assistance in addition to preliminary admission. Many of these students are currently enrolled in programs in these universities, while many former participants have earned graduate and professional degrees.

The Social Science Student Schools (4-S) program was a model honors program for our most intelligent and motivated social science majors, with at least junior status. All 4-S students (approximately 30 per year, for four years, 1980-1984) were enrolled in a contemporary topics course which truly sharpened their listening, writing, speaking, and thinking skills. The course was team taught, and the class interaction was a real preview of a graduate class. Most of these participants were very successful in both graduate and professional schools. This project was funded by a Lilly Endowment, Inc. Foundation award, which served as a prototype to our expanded and expanding honors program.

--**Harold Conley**, professor of psychology and assistant vice president for academic affairs

During the Harvey administration, there have been many significant events, innovations and changes within the School of Nursing.

The School of Nursing held its first "Agency Colloquium" with 25 representatives of the various clinical agencies with whom it had contractual arrangements during the 1980-81 academic year. The colloquium served as a vehicle for informing those vital constituencies about the future directions planned for the School of Nursing. It also provided agency personnel with an opportunity to provide input and exchange ideas regarding future cooperative endeavors. The dean of the School of Nursing initiated a faculty mentorship program to enhance the orientation of new faculty appointed to the school. This procedure enabled new faculty members to become acclimated to their new academic environment and the organizational culture of the School of Nursing in a more timely manner. . .A researcher-in-residence was appointed to the School of Nursing in 1989, and collaborating with the School of Nursing faculty, estab-

lished a research agenda for the school.
>   --**Elnora Daniel**, dean of the School of Nursing (1980-91) and vice president for academic affairs (July 1991-)

The change in structure and the change in name led to more visibility for the entire university. Specifically, the change brought great visibility to the graduate programs at Hampton University. It placed a small school or program, the Graduate College, in a leadership position. The dean was elected to the board of directors of the Council of Graduate Schools; and as the first woman president of the Conference of Southern Graduate Schools. . .Graduate leadership at Hampton has produced outstanding graduates, has contributed to the arena of graduate education in this country and abroad and has kept the program at the forefront of graduate education. Finally, it has been highly successful in acquiring external funds.
>   --**Hazel Garrison**, former dean of The Graduate College (1977-1990), former assistant vice president for research and professor emeritus of biology

There were five major changes during my tenure that I believe have changed the character of the university:

Restructuring of the institution from Hampton Institute (1984) to Hampton University (1985)

Establishment of the College of Continuing Education (1984)

Establishment of the Teaching Learning Technology Center (1985)

Establishment of the Center for Teaching Excellence (1988)

Establishment of innovative programs within the College of Continuing Education.

The College of Continuing Education has been from its inception an innovative entity of the university. Its primary focus has been to provide challenging, marketable and highly visible programs that are attractive to the adult. It has used high technology as a means not only of expanding the educational tools available to adults, but also as a way of increasing its student population. The College of Continuing Education now serves students from every state within the United States and four European countries.

--**Willie O. Lawton**, dean, College of Continuing Education

Our Assessment Facilitator Program gives the Center for Teaching Excellence an opportunity to work closely with 15 of our best, most effective faculty on an intensive basis so that they improve their skills and become more attractive advertisements for our programs.

Feedback that we receive from faculty indicates that the Center for Teaching Excellence has had a significant impact on their interactions with students. They indicate that they are engaging in instructional encounters with students with an entirely different frame of mind, that they are conscious of their students in completely new ways, consequently relating to the teaching-learning process in a wholly changed way.

--**Linda Petty**, director, Center for Teaching Excellence

Activities which significantly changed the character of the university were the change from Institute to University, implementation of the Presidential Eminent Scholars Program, creation of the Academic

Support Center, development of the Computer Science Program, and the development of the Airway Science Program.

>   --**Oscar Prater**, former vice president for administrative services (1979-1990) and president, Fort Valley State University (1990 -)

One of the most important innovations that has greatly altered the character of Hampton University is the introduction of academic computing in various departments.

The feedback from employers of our students shows praise for our students' ability to use microcomputers in their professions. In fact, some students have attributed their success in obtaining positions in corporations to their computing background... The department has exhibited considerable success, during the decade under review, in graduating over ninety percent of the students who entered the university with declared majors in economics. Approximately 40 percent of our students go on to graduate schools like the Wharton School of Business, The College of William and Mary, University of Michigan, University of Rochester and Howard University, just to mention a few. About 25 percent of the students go to law school, and the remaining 35 percent work in various business fields and in the government sector.

Hampton University is gradually growing in reputation. Its prestige factor is similar to mainstream institutions like Harvard and MIT. It is also becoming a center with multiculturally and ethnically diverse faculty, placing us in a unique position to exploit the coming global opportunities the nation will be encountering.

>   --**Ayuba Sarki** chair, department of economics, School of Business

A Legacy of Innovations

From its early beginnings Hampton has been in the forefront of pre-school and elementary education. During a period in American higher education when most colleges were abdicating their responsibility to pre-college pupils, Hampton continued to support and expand its laboratory schools.

The Early Childhood Laboratory School evolved in 1930 to provide training for teachers of young children. Additionally, it focused on educational, physical and social development for pre-school children. The Hampton University Non-graded Laboratory School (a continuous progress innovation) was founded in 1962 as an adjunct to the Department of Elementary Education. Both the Early Childhood Laboratory School and the Non-graded Laboratory School became national models in their fields and models for educational change in the decade of the eighties.

While many universities gave up their laboratory schools during the eighties, Hampton continued its commitment and legacy of serving the pre-college generation at the early levels of the educational continuum, thereby providing both a clinical setting and model for education majors and in-service educators-- and an innovative teaching and learning environment for school-age children. This leadership stance taken by Hampton resulted in increased numbers of externally and internally funded projects.

Laboratory School Outreach

Julia G. Williams, director, Hampton University Laboratory School (1972-1989; 1990-91)

In 1980, James Victor, associate director for the National Center for Minority Special Education Research and Outreach, received a Department of Education grant for the implementation of the Hampton Institute Mainstreaming Model (HIMM) which became an integral component of the Early Childhood Division of the Hampton University Laboratory School. This was the only facility in the Hampton community to admit handicapped pre-schoolers into a mainstreamed classroom environment providing professional services including resources, consultants, teachers professionally trained in special education and mainstreaming. A comprehensive developmental assessment and individualized educational program was designed for each child. Further we established a parental support program including workshops and conferences. Students majoring in special education and in early childhood education received on-site experiences in working with the special education pre-schoolers in a mainstreamed environment.

Project Leap

The Learning Experiences for Assessing Potential project was a cooperative effort between the Hampton University Laboratory School and Hampton City Schools. LEAP sought to identify and assess students who may have high potential not observable easily through traditional evaluation techniques. The Early Childhood Center in the Hampton University Laboratory School served as a demonstration site for the program. Laboratory School pupils joined students from Hampton city schools in the Pull-Out Program designed to expand problem-solving abilities and creative thinking. Multiple disciplines were integrated in order to encourage the development of productive, abstract, high-level thinking skills.

Kiddie Kollege & Kiddie Kamp

"Kiddie Kollege" was created in 1981 as an extension of the laboratory school to provide enrichment activities for children during the months of June and July. The program included reading, language arts, arts and crafts, instrumental music, computer skills, library training, dramatics, science exploration, journalism, Spanish, typing and mathematical problem-solving.

In 1983, "Kiddie Kamp" was added to "Kiddie Kollege" as an afternoon day camp program with planned activities in swimming, sports and games, weekly field trips, a parent-counselor evening and an overnight camp experience. Kiddie Kamp was sponsored by the Department of Health, Physical Education and Recreation.

"Kiddie Kollege-Kiddie Kamp" had a tremendous impact throughout Hampton, Newport News and surrounding areas as well as nationwide. Children came from as far away as Georgia, New York, Texas and even California. In fact, several summer participants from as many as 16 states attended. The program offered something for all children ages five through 12. The participants were heterogeneous in socio-economic status, skill development, cultural and racial background, and scholastic achievements.

The fact that Hampton maintained the Laboratory School during the eighties and into the nineties reflects the university's commitment to providing a sound education to children and youth, as well as those of college age and beyond.

Retention Is Critical to the Future

From the time students step on the campus until they graduate, they have access to a support network designed to make academic success easier to attain. Specifically charged with student retention, the Assessment and Learning Support Center, founded in 1981, has focused on the academic retention of freshmen with deficient academic backgrounds. According to Peggy Wallace, director, the center employs a holistic approach to improve academic retention by fostering an environment in which the student's academic, career and personal needs are met.

Through the years the Assessment and Learning Support Center has incorporated many services within the unit, including these:

University 101--The Individual and Life	Program planning
Diagnostic and prescriptive services	Developmental courses in reading, English and mathematics
Education 295--Learning to Learn	Counseling services
Academic advisement	Student support services.

Finally, it can be said that the well-designed program and services of the center have led to improvement in student retention.

1990 Student Retention Award

The Hampton University Assessment and Learning Support Center was awarded a 1990 Retention Excellence Award at the July 1990, National Conference on Student Retention in Washington, D.C. In the words of the conference organizers, "The Retention Excellence Awards were established to honor the most creative and effective of the approaches at regionally accredited post-secondary educational institutions throughout North America."

Among the 24 colleges selected to receive this award were the University of Virginia, the University of Illinois, Clemson University, Loyola University, and Baylor University. Hampton University was the only historically black institution honored.

National Treasures--University Archives and Museum

Believing in the use of concrete examples in the teaching-learning process, General Samuel Chapman Armstrong secured artifacts from his home in Hawaii to be used as instructional aides. And the University Museum had its beginning. Similarly, both the general and the Northern missionaries who were the first teachers and administrators at Hampton were extremely sensitive to the historical significance of the post-Civil War era. Therefore, letters, documents and issues of the *Southern Workman* were kept, and these invaluable records of the Hampton Normal and Agricultural Institute led to the establishment of the university's archives.

Fritz Malval, university archivist, is well aware of the history. According to him, in March 1967, Paul Gates, chair of the department of history at Cornell University; Lester J. Cappan, historian and former archivist of Colonial Williamsburg, and Edith Mead Fox, former curator and university archivist, Cornell University, were invited to report on the institution's holdings in connection with the establishment and organization of Hampton Institute's Archives.

The three consultants noted the importance and necessity of instituting an archives project in order to preserve and make available for research the various collections of papers. In his report, Fox stated, "Hampton Institute has an impressive number of records documenting its history stored away in various locations on campus. But these most precious records are all ill-housed and ill-kept, despite the evident respect of them. Many of those most precious to Hampton's history are crammed into the overflowing president's vault where the hot, dry, dead air is good neither for the records nor researcher."

It was within the background of the Fox report that in 1972, materials were moved from nooks and crannies around the campus and placed on the third floor of the new addition of the Collis P. Huntington Memorial Library.

From Obscurity to Prominence

The archival holdings became a collection of national prominence during the 1978-1991 era, and a guide to these holdings was published with funds from a National Endowment for the Humanities grant. This five-volume *Guide to Hampton Institute Archives* was reviewed in the *American Archivist* by Harold T. Pinkett who stated, "It is one of the most detailed finding aids that has been compiled concerning the archival holdings of an American educational institution...The guide is also one of the most detailed compilations providing access to a large body of archival materials concerning important aspects of black and native American history."

The archival holdings have become a valuable research facility for students and faculty. Beginning in 1980, a system for providing research service to scholars was developed, and currently students and researchers come from all over the nation to conduct research, write articles, papers, theses, dissertations and books. According to Malval, "The archives are known as an excellent Research Center all over the world, particularly England, Finland, Hawaii, Japan, South Africa, Switzerland and Zimbabwe."

Renowned Collection Grows

Hampton University's Museum has always been recognized as a

valuable historical resource. Established in 1888 as a support to the academic programs, it continues to serve that function today. However, under the leadership of Jeanne Zeidler, the museum has become one of the nation's acclaimed multicultural educational resources.

Through a number of grants from such agencies like the National Endowment of the Arts, the Ford Foundation, and the Virginia Foundation for the Arts, the university has been able to design a multifaceted plan for preservation, acquisition and education. Accordingly, Hampton has invested substantial funds to maintain and enhance the rich cultural legacy of the museum. The Graduate College instituted a master's degree program in archival and museum studies. Under this curriculum, students pursuing the museum option have interned at the Hampton University Museum. All graduates, by the way, have moved into museum positions in various parts of the nation.

In his 1991 annual report, William Harvey reported accordingly:

> *Excellence is sought by Hampton University in every area of its programs and operations. However, to achieve distinction is only the beginning, for excellence is a continuing process of maintaining quality and superiority. This recognition has guided a very significant and very successful program of collection development at the Hampton University Museum. Through a combination of carefully considered purchases and gifts from numerous donors, the museum collection has grown during my administration in the last 13 years.*
>
> *Since 1978, more than 1,700 pieces have been added to the Museum collection, bringing the total holdings to over 9,000 artifacts and works of art....*
>
> *In 1868, when Hampton's founder and first president, General Samuel Chapman Armstrong, began the Museum at Hampton Normal and Agricultural Institute, he wrote, "I wish to make and to have here the finest collection in the U.S. I think that by taking pains I can beat the other collections in this country." Dur-*

> *ing the thirteen years of my tenure, I am pleased that Hampton University maintained this tradition of quality, thereby ensuring the transformation of Armstrong's wish into realty. . . . This extraordinary accomplishment could not have been achieved without the guiding hand and leadership of Ms. Jeanne Zeidler, director of the Hampton University Museum since 1980.*

During the 1978-1991 era, the collections have been classified into five major groups--African, Fine Arts, American Indian, Hampton University History, and Asian Pacific. Outstanding new acquisitions include works by Harlem Renaissance artists, additional Tanner paintings, Elizabeth Catlett, Charles White, John Biggers, Samella Lewis, and Ron Adams. Broken down by collection, acquisitions over this period can be listed accordingly:

Hampton University History 302		Asian Pacific 147
American Indian 94	Fine Arts 395	African 878

During the 1978-1991 period, the Hampton University Museum became an invaluable educational resource for university students, public school pupils, and national and international scholars.

Summary

Academics were indeed the critical components of the educational enterprise at Hampton University between 1978 and 1991. It was during this time that:

- The university made a transition from a small college to a comprehensive university.
- A series of innovative new programs were introduced in the Undergraduate College, the Graduate College and the College of Continuing Education.
- The faculty assumed prominence in research in their disciplines at national and international levels.

- The School of Pure and Applied Sciences became a growing entity in research.
- The School of Business became one of the largest academic units.
- The School of Nursing assumed leadership in providing health care services in low-income communities and training in Africa and Central America.
- The School of Arts and Letters and the School of Education were merged into one unit and became the School of Liberal Arts and Education.
- The dean of the Graduate College became the first representative of a historically black college to assume presidency of the Southern Association of Graduate Schools.
- The College of Continuing Education introduced degree-granting programs to non-traditional students.
- An innovative freshman studies program and a revised general education program were institutionalized.
- The Assessment and Learning Support Center, the University Museum and University Archives rose to national and international prominence.

Academics have been and always will be the most important business of Hampton University.

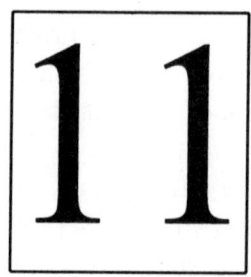

FACULTY, STAFF, STUDENTS AND ALUMNI ACCEPT THE CHALLENGE OF CHANGE

My goal has been to document the administrative and operational procedures that had a significant impact on Hampton University as it changed in both structure and substance from 1978 to 1992.

The success or failure of any enterprise is to a large degree reflected in the perspective of those who are actively involved in its operation. In fact, the faculty and staff at Hampton may have an entirely different perspective than mine.

What did faculty and staff really think about the challenges they faced as the Hampton University higher education model evolved over this critical era? To gain some insight, we distributed a questionnaire to members of the college community and other selected individuals who were part of the 1991 administrative retreat.

We sought answers to questions that addressed innovation and leadership:

1. Identify events, innovations, and/or changes that you feel significantly altered the character of the university.

2. Describe the role you and others under your supervision played in carrying out these changes.
3. What benefits, if any, resulted from these events, innovations and changes?

There was also an attempt to gain insight into the challenges that administrators faced during this period. We asked these questions:

1. What do you feel have been the greatest challenges faced in your area during the years 1978-1991?
2. How did you resolve or respond to the challenges?
3. What influence, if any, did these challenges and your response have on the growth and development of students, faculty, administrators and the university at large?

From these questions, we obtained the following responses.

Computerization of the Archives

Computerization of archival holdings was identified by Fritz Malval, university archivist as the greatest challenge. He asserted, "The introduction of new technology, information databases and the yearly avalanche of information made it necessary to provide basic training in the utilization of technology to those who offer archival services. The resolution to the challenge was met through the AT&T and Bell Laboratories Library Network Summer Mentoring Program. As a result, archival personnel became proficient in using the archival database."

Scholarships for Bright Students

Oscar Prater, former vice president for administrative services, felt that the need to attract superior students was one of his major challenges, resolved through the implementation of the Presidential Eminent Scholars Program.

Library Services

Throughout the period in question there were ongoing concerns about the library. "I have felt for a long time that our library was not what it should be," states Cora Reid, a library staff member... "It was a great day for me when I heard the construction of the library was going to begin. I feel that the university library is finally on the way to becoming an outstanding library [since] we've moved into our new facility."

Student Facilities

Alexander Strawn, former dean of students, points out that the shortage of campus housing units "had been a major problem at Hampton University for several years. This problem was attacked by the provision of additional housing units and expanding and upgrading housing services." He also suggested that the movement of health services from a building that had been partially condemned to the beautiful remodeled St. Cyprian's church building "had a tremendously positive effect on the campus community."

Teacher Education

Mary T. Christian, delegate to Virginia General Assembly and former dean of the School of Education says that the period in which she assumed leadership was one in which the School of Education saw a drastic decline in enrollment in teacher education. This challenge was addressed through the combining of the departments of elementary and early childhood education. The new configuration established the department of elementary education with two teacher-endorsement areas: early childhood NK-4 and intermediate 4-7. In order to maintain the rich legacy of the school, Dr. Christian sought assistance from alumni of the school and educators who had been educated by Eva C. Mitchell, a pioneer in elementary education, and William H. Robinson, a recognized scholar in philosophy and history of education. The Eva C. Mitchell Endowed Scholarship was established to assist outstanding students majoring in teacher education, and an annual William H. Robinson Lecture Series brought outstanding speakers to the campus. These innovations played a significant role in maintaining the prestige of an area which throughout the history of the university had enjoyed a national reputation for excellence.

External Challenge

In 1987, Carlton Brown assumed leadership as the new dean of the School of Education. His challenge was to increase enrollment and to address the new mandates from the state department of education requiring all colleges and universities in the Commonwealth of Virginia to restructure their teacher education programs. These mandates for the most part eliminated elementary education as a major by requiring that all teachers select liberal arts or science areas as a major discipline.

The faculty and the dean of the school devised a teacher-education model that not only met the state mandate, but also enabled the unit to be accepted for membership in the prestigious Holmes Group--a consortium of more than 100 major schools of education.

Combining Schools

As vice president for academic affairs, I saw that state requirement as an opportunity to encourage the faculty in the arts and sciences to assume more responsibility for the knowledge base of future teachers. Consequently, when there was a vacancy for the dean of arts and letters, it was recommended to the president that the two units be combined, and in 1990 Carlton Brown became dean of the School of Liberal Arts and Education. The new configuration led to both increased enrollment and students of higher quality pursuing teacher education.

Business School Explosion

The greatest enrollment numbers in the contemporary period has been in the School of Business. Edward Pyatt, who served as chair of the department of finance and interim dean of the School of Business, indicated that the greatest challenge before the school in this period was the rapid enrollment from 800 students to over 1500. We expected that this growth would create problems. But additional difficulties were created by the turnover of top administrators.

To stabilize the school, Hampton University, like other institutions, found that it had to compete in a buyer's market. The establishment of a differential marketplace salary scale was utilized to recruit and maintain salaries. In addition, the president set up a special scholarship fund that provided financial assistance to faculty members who pursued the Ph.D. degree at regional universities while maintaining a reduced teaching load.

The crises in the School of Business were also addressed by the establishment of an advisement and counseling center within the school. The counselors worked with faculty advisors to facilitate the goals of students within the School of Business.

Alumni Affairs

During this period, the university received strong support from its alumni in recruitment and fund raising. Many of the students are sons and daughters of the alumni as well as students recruited by Hampton graduates in the local and regional associations. During this period of rapid growth, several changes were begun, some of which were of concern to the alumni. Vivian David, alumni director, said that resistance to change for some alumni was an internal and external challenge. She said that it was difficult for the office of alumni affairs to help those alumni who were nostalgic about the university to accept the many changes taking place.

It was in this period that the alumni association became incorporated. Through the joint efforts of the committee of both the university board of trustees and the National Hampton Alumni Association, the two groups resolved differences. David says that Hampton University "has a very strong alumni association that supports the goals and mission of the institution," adding "The pre-alumni clubs in the undergraduate college are steadily growing and represent the foundation upon which a strong national organization will continually be built."

Technology Invades the University

Throughout the 1978-1992 era, Hampton University was an institution on the move. From the appointment of the new president in March 1978 to the end of the 1991 academic year, administrators and faculty introduced countless innovative approaches and strategies that altered the operational character of the institution. According to Ayuba Sarki, chair of the department of economics, "The most important innovation that greatly changed the character of Hampton University was the introduction of academic computing in the teaching and learning environment. . ." It is important to recognize the speed with which the vice president for academic affairs responded with this technological innovation to the invitation of consultants during the annual post-session activities. The establishment of the Teaching Learning Technology Center marked the foothold of academic computing at the university.

Earl Bean, director of libraries, considered the introduction of technology in the Huntington Library and additional technology in the new Harvey Library to be an innovation that influenced significantly the quantity and quality of library services. He suggested: "When Hampton University joined the On-line Computer Library Center (OCLC) in 1985, it enabled the library to share cataloging with other libraries throughout the nation. The introduction of C/D ROM computer-based technology gave Hampton University library patrons greater access to periodicals, indices, abstracts, selected references and other educational materials. A move to the new, fully computerized library in 1991 was an innovation that changed the academic potential of the university for today and tomorrow."

The university registrar saw the changes in registration procedures as an improvement for the university. After being associated with five other registrars before assuming the post, Jorsene Cooper stated: "The registrar's office has improved its registration from each student signing a class list in Phenix Hall, on the second floor, along with the registrar's staff pulling computer cards for each student for each course and collecting these cards and submitting them to the computer center for processing, to an on-the-phone registration system. In 1991, students could use the telephone to enter their courses into the system from home or campus using a touchtone telephone. This eliminated the waiting in line for a key operator to enter courses. The phone registration system can also notify the student when a course is closed, about a course conflict, whether another section is available, if a student is not admitted, and if a student is financially or academically cleared."

Establishment of the Honors College

Among the innovations that significantly altered the character of the university was the establishment of the Honors College within the undergraduate college. Honors dorms were created, and those selected for residence received a reduction in housing fees in recognition of their academic success. Implementing a complete honors curriculum continues to be a challenge.

Eleanor Lynch, first director of Honors College, indicated that the greatest challenges in honors from 1986-1991 were to encourage the faculty to develop a variety of course options (seminars and colloquia, for example) to adapt to the special needs of gifted students. The problem was not lack of desire or interest, but the time required to accomplish the tasks. Despite the lack of volume in terms of options completed, the idea of educational opportunities for gifted students was important to the university.

Special Preparation for Graduate School

In addition to the honors program, there were numerous opportunities for students to extend themselves beyond the limits of the regular classroom. The department of political science witnessed phenomenal growth during this period, and made it a part of its programmatic focus to prepare its majors for graduate school.

According to Hoda Zaki, department of political science chairperson, "The percentage of graduating seniors who entered graduate or professional schools varies from 30% in 1986 to 67% in 1990. Preparation for graduate school was enhanced through a number of departmental activities such as having the majors to become involved in simulation programs of the United Nations, Organization of African Unity and the Arab League hosted by Old Dominion University, Howard University and American University. Students also participate in summer programs supported by the American Political Science Association, Woodrow Wilson Foundation, Duke University and others. In addition, the department presented national conferences including Philanthropy and Afro-American Higher Education in the 20th Century."

A University in Bloom

During this contemporary era, one might compare Hampton University to the arrival of spring. Like nature pulling forth spring plants in many varieties, this institution nurtured change and diversity among local, regional, national and international establishments, individuals and groups.

Many activities enriched the lives of children and youth, young adults and senior citizens, Americans, Asians, Africans, Europeans, Central Americans, South Americans and islanders--in other words, individuals and groups throughout planet earth. The impact of the institution has not been limited to the trustees, administration, faculty, staff, students, alumni, parents, friends or curriculum or any single event or person. Like spring, Hampton has been busting out all over.

Following is a capsule review bringing into focus renowned speakers, local state, national and international leaders, visual and performing artists, writers and poets who have added to the richness of the Hampton University environment. The Hampton University landscape included stellar events and individuals, hundreds of people and events, including the board of trustees, endowment management, administrative development, visiting and performing artists, university productions, distinguished scholars, international visitors and many more. In addition to faculty, students, staff, alumni, and administration, Hampton's success and growth was a result of these people and events.

Trustee Leadership

The board of trustees under the leadership of James Henderson, Ray LaFlore and the current chairman, Wendell Holmes assumed its stewardship through active involvement in committees which included academic affairs, board relationships, student affairs, alumni affairs, finance, physical plant, and development. In addition, these gentlemen served on *ad hoc* committees as well as the important executive committee.

Members of the board of trustees were among America's top corporate executives, national education leaders and state and national political leaders.

Endowment Investment

The president in collaboration with the board of trustees formed a profit-making corporation. Among the undertakings of this independent corporation was the building of Hampton Harbor. This endeavor includes the construction of 240 apartment units and a shopping mall on university property.

Historical Excavation

Unexpectedly, the 1989 excavation for Hampton Harbor uncovered a colonial settlement with a brick cellar, trash pits, crafts and many colonial artifacts. A prehistoric Indian site was also uncovered by an anthropology team. Artifacts from both excavations have been added to the vast collection in the university museum.

Administrative Retreats

Administrative retreats were established by President Harvey to give his council, deans, chairs, and unit heads an opportunity to assess critically and evaluate the status of the university and to address current issues. The three-day retreats were held at Nags Head, North Carolina and Hilton Head, South Carolina. The administrative development workshops served to keep the administrators on the cutting edge of higher education.

International Legacy

Continuous efforts to maintain the university's position in international affairs were undertaken by selected academic units. Fulbright Scholars, diplomats and foreign dignitaries were an integral part of activity at the university. Among those who shared their insights with the academic community were:

> **Honorable Gertrude Mongella**
> Minister of State, Office of the Prime Minister of Tanzania. In 1991 Mongella became Tanzania's Ambassador to India.
>
> **Honorable Lindiwe Mabuza**
> Chief Representative of the African National Congress to the U.S.
>
> **Mr. Papie Moloto**
> African National Congress Administrative Secretary
>
> **Mr. Andre Kortunov,**
> Russian Scholar, department of foreign policy of the Institute for the Study of United States and Canadian Studies

Art in the Making

Hampton University continues to be a culture center in the Tidewater area of Virginia. It was a special treat for the community to be benefactors of the creative talents of **Ed Hamilton** who was the sculptor for the life-size statue of Booker T. Washington.

John Biggers one of America's famous artists and a student at Hampton during his early college days, spent a year in residency creating the magnificent murals that grace the entrance of the Harvey Library. While in residence, he worked with students and faculty, and shared his works with the Hampton community.

Visual and Performing Artists

Hampton University has always been a cultural center for the Virginia Peninsula. The students, faculty and the community have had the opportunity to witness performances by America's outstanding artists, including these:

Maya Angelou--national poet, author and actress; She thrilled audiences in Ogden Hall on her several visits as speaker for the installation of student leaders.

Ernest Gaines--award winning author; Gaines came to Hampton at the climax of the annual Read-In. His novel, *A Gathering of Old Men* was the focus of the read-in.

Toni Morrison--Nobel Prize-winning author and 20th century literary great conducted workshops and fascinated audiences.

Gwendolyn Brooks--Pulitzer Prize-winning Poet Laureate of Illinois, established an annual poet writing contest for university students. She was the featured artist of the 1991 Poetry Festival.

The Writers-in-Residence program enabled the entire academic community to interact with and enjoy other literary notables like **Margaret Burroughs, Amiri Baraka** (LeRoi Jones), **Sonia Sanchez, Alice Childress** and others.

Television star and actor **Lou Gossett, Jr.** appeared on the Ogden Hall stage to share anecdotes with the audience about his role in the movie version of *A Gathering of Old Men*.

For over a decade, the annual Young Authors Conference provided an opportunity for the children from the University Laboratory School and surrounding communities to be introduced to renowned authors like **Katherine Paterson, Ann Martin** and **Thomas Rockwell**.

Distinguished Visitors

Departments, schools and the university itself sought to provide the students with a broad education through lecture series, national conferences and a distinguished visitors program. Among the notables who contributed to the university environment were:

> **Arthur Ashe**--Wimbledon tennis winner
> **Ruby Dee** and **Ossie Davis**--noted lecturers and actors
> **Dr. Thomas Tobi**--1981 Nobel Laureate in economics
> **Dr. Vincent Hardy**--noted theologian
> **Summer Murray**--Pulitzer Prize journalist
> **Honorable L. Douglas Wilder**--Virginia's first black governor
> **Rev. Jesse Jackson**--civil rights activist
> **Dr. C. Eric Lincoln**--noted professor of religion and culture, Duke University
> **Dr. John N. Gardner**--renowned educator, University of South Carolina
> **President George Bush**--President of the United States and 1991 commencement speaker
> **Ronald Brown**--chairman, Democratic National Committee, 1992 commencement speaker (current U.S. Secretary of Commerce)

Music in the Air

The university and local community looked forward to *The Messiah* conducted by Hampton University's own Roland Carter. The production provided an opportunity for Carter's university choir not only to showcase their talents but also to work with renowned vocalists like **William Warfield, George Shirley** and Hampton faculty member **Marilyn Thompson.**

Hampton University Is a Mosaic

Hampton University is truly a mosaic of people, events and programs. The section on the university in review is a sampling of some of the events which have been a part of the Hampton scene.

Still, the complexity of the institution is reflected in the challenges and innovations which have been presented in this and previous chapters. This contemporary history is but a capsule view of a historically black college that has met the challenge of providing educational excellence to its students and contributing to the nation and the global marketplace. I say this is a living history because the administration, faculty, and students of this renowned institution continue to face new challenges.

Perhaps the best reflection of the future of Hampton University is the charge President Harvey gave to the class of 1991 and the senior class president's response to that challenge.

CHARGE TO THE GRADUATING CLASS OF 1991
Ogre Phi Ogre VII
by President William R. Harvey

Today, you are among many young men and women across the nation who have reached a significant milestone in their lives. You have toiled long and hard for this day. In the years ahead, you must be able to say that your efforts have not been in vain. From this point in your life, you must work even harder to achieve the goals you have set for your future.

During your tenure here, the administration, faculty and staff have attempted to demonstrate to you the need for a total education--wholeness of knowledge--the ability to know *how to think* rather than merely *what to think*.

Knowing how to think is a crucial skill for survival in these times and for the future. The world is full of diversities, and your success in life may well be predicated upon your ability to think and discern for yourselves what is best for you, rather than relying on what others may design for you.

Recalling W.E.B. DuBois' attempt to define why we need college, he stated that college develops "that fine adjustment between life and the growing knowledge of life, an adjustment which forms the secret of civilization." As you set out to achieve your future goals, remember that education is a never ending process in which one strives to make a fine adjustment, or a refitting of a body of knowledge in a world where real life is forever changing.

Your stay at Hampton University has been preparation for the future which requires you to be a humanitarian, an intellectual, and a utilitarian. I challenge you to maintain honor, dignity, decency and concern for mankind, as you leave these hallowed halls and strive to live up to the demands of one who is educated.

It is my hope that here you have been inspired to participate in lifelong learning; to be concerned about shaping the future and not be dull and drab practitioners of what is or has been. I challenge you to be change agents and catalysts who will provide strong moral leadership and create a world of greater justice, beauty and goodwill. Fight bigotry and racism whenever and wherever it raises its ugly head. Remember that it comes in all shapes, forms and fashions . . . sometimes even disguised as a friend.

Promote economic development and economic independence. Develop the habits of saving and investing. Economic prosperity will take you farther than a political, social or other agenda.

Remember to always support your *alma mater*. Support the programs and people of the university, for these people provided you with the tools to be all that you can be.

As you leave our *Home by the Sea*, remember that you are responsible for sustaining the legacy of the Hampton dynasty. So I now charge you, members of the Class of 1991, to don your shield of power, strength and unity, and let your lives do the singing through the service that will reverberate for centuries to come.

RESPONSE TO PRESIDENT HARVEY'S CHALLENGE
by Senior Class President Carvel Lewis

Dr. Harvey, the graduating Class of 1991 cheerfully and confidently accepts your challenge to achieve excellence in its highest forms. Hampton University, a standard of excellence, has prepared us to accept this great challenge.

We shall remain eternally grateful to the faculty, administration and staff for helping to prepare us for the opportunities and challenges that now beckon to us. We are also grateful to the employees of our buildings and grounds department for contributing to our comfort and security during our tenure here.

On this grand occasion and in this place, we gladly accept the full mantle of adulthood. Across America and around the world, we stand ready to continue to learn, to lead, and to serve. As artists, architects, engineers, educators, scientists, managers of businesses, and health care professionals, we seek the opportunities, challenges, and responsibilities that the world promises us.

As we leave this place of inspiration and learning, we will enter careers, eager to make positive contributions to the development of the peoples of the world. We now stand ready to educate the youth, to create great works of art, to advance the frontiers of science and technology, to promote ethics in business, to preserve our natural environment, and to serve our government in peace and in war.

President Bush, you honor us with your presence at and your participation in our commencement. We shall remember this day--the occasion of our rite of passage--until we are "old and gray and full of sleep."

Mr. President, please consider us your "thousand points of light." The thousand members of this graduating class reaffirm our faith in "the land of the free and the home of the brave." Exercising our constitutional and civil rights as citizens of this great democracy, we shall always cherish and defend our rights of "life, liberty, and the pursuit of happiness," as long as the country does the same for us.

We live in the world, and we shall make this world a better place to live.

Members of this dedicated and distinguished faculty, we shall always remember--we shall never forget--the great lessons we have learned about truth, goodness, and beauty. We shall continue to apply what we have learned as we depart for the hallowed halls of graduate and professional schools, in the science laboratories, in the executive offices of business and government, on the athletic and battle fields, in libraries and museums, in sacred places of meditation and worship--wherever we go and whatever we do, we shall continue to strive for excellence.

We will make Hampton University proud of us, and we shall always remain proud of "our *Home by the Sea*."

We deeply appreciate the support and love that our parents, relatives, and friends have given us through the years. Thank you for helping to make our graduation possible.

We heartily accept the great challenge before us. Our time has come! This is the day that the Lord has made. Let us rejoice and be glad in it.

EPILOGUE

Where Do We Go From Here?

I have presented a documentary case study of the inner workings of this university during a critical period in the history of higher education. Public confidence in higher education began to drop. Certain societal and political issues like the downturn in the nation's economy had an impact not only on all of higher education but also on--and to a greater degree--historically black colleges and universities. The political push for ethnic diversity in the nation's flagship colleges and universities resulted in a brain drain of minority professionals, and the bidder's market for the best and brightest minority secondary school graduates forced Hampton University to compete in the larger academic arena for faculty and students.

I have tried to document those factors which contributed to the survival and unprecedented growth of the university during the first 12 years of the presidency of William R. Harvey: 1978-1991. It was during this period that the faculty, students, staff and administrators developed a higher education model which enabled the university to expand and become a symbol of excellence in the global academic marketplace. However, even with a glorious legacy Hampton University must meet the ever increasing challenges of a fluid society. In order to maintain its rightful place among other outstanding institutions of higher education, the faculty, staff, administration and trustees at Hampton University must first have a vision and a plan for the future.

A number of respondents to the survey used to collect data for this documentary history provided me with vision statements. Here are the responses to the question, "Describe the university as you currently see it. Give special attention to your area and what you would like future generations to know."

> *Hampton University is an institution well established in higher education throughout the state, nation and world. It is greatly respected for its educational programs, its administration, its faculty and its*

staff. While it has tradition as its epoxy, Hampton is also dynamic, vibrant and evolving into an even greater institution.
>--Earl Bean,
>Director of Libraries

Hampton University has undergone remarkable changes within the period 1978-92. Within the School of Pure and Applied Sciences special attention has been given to the development of programs that will receive national recognition for their excellence. It is felt that several departments have already gained the kind of reputation that will enable them to attract high ability students who, upon graduation, will find many opportunities for continuing their education in professional and graduate schools. And in those disciplines where the undergraduate professional degrees are awarded, our students will be sought out as a select group for employment.
>--Robert Bonner

I see the evolution of the university searching for and refining its role in the area of higher education. As we work together to sort out and commit ourselves to strengthening our programs and deleting programs and services that do not relate to the current mission, it is easy to see that Hampton can retain its tradition of uniqueness and continue to produce quality scientists, musicians, teachers, Army and Navy professionals, nurses, athletes, artists, media professionals, interior designers, architects, sculptors, air traffic control specialists, computer specialists, speech pathologists, interpreters, and a host of other highly qualified professionals.
>--Rufus Easter,
>Director of Auxillary Services

The university is a living breathing being of scholarship. Like a multi-celled animal it has component parts, students, faculty etc. without which this multi-celled being dies. The library acts as the nervous system of the university allowing the university to build memory (the Library's collection) and acting as sensory organs which allows the being to intercommunicate with its parts and to the outside... As the world of scholarly endeavour changes and modes of communication and instruction change the Library must remain in the forefront abreast of these changes. Because it serves scholarship in the broadest sense, unfettered by disciplinary squabbles, etc., it performs its function to all scholarship and should tend to overcome walls that separate the divisions of learning.
--Frank Edgecomb,
Librarian

I see Hampton University as a university which has great potential if there is full acceptance and an understanding that structurally, there are three distinct units; The Undergraduate College; The Graduate College; and the College of Continuing Education.. .I would like to see the university recognize fully graduate education for what it is and that a university must have a strong graduate unit with a graduate faculty active in research and grantsmanship. . . . I would like future generations to know that in spite of obstacles, the graduate leadership at Hampton has produced outstanding graduates, has contributed to the arena of graduate education in this country and abroad and has kept the program at the forefront of graduate education.
--Hazel Garrison,
Professor Emeritus and
retired Dean of the Graduate
College

> *The university today finds the age-old concept of "Education for Life" highly adaptable to life's changing conditions which have become challenges of the twenty-first century...Future alumni generations should be ever knowledgeable of the role they must be prepared to play in support of the university as we lay the groundwork today for this preparation.*
>
> --Alphonso Knight,
> Former Director of Alumni Affairs and Former President, National Hampton Alumni Affairs

> *I feel that the university has not yet reached its academic potential. Higher academic plateaus are within our reach. However, I would not like to see the university grow to such numbers that we will lose our uniqueness and family-like atmosphere. The Hampton story is still unfolding.*
>
> --Barbara Lamb,
> Librarian

> *The phasing in of new faculty members and key administrators has caused a new wave of thinking among the university family. The university's emphasis upon international education and multi-cultural involvement are good indicators that the university is shifting its focus from what was to what should be as we move toward the 21st century. The College of Continuing Education has been, from its inception, an innovative entity of the university. Its primary focus has been upon providing challenging, marketable and high visible programs that are attractive to the adult. It has used high technology as a means of expanding the educational tools available to adults, as well as increasing its student population. The College of Continuing Education now serves students from every*

state within the United States and four European countries.

--Willie Lawton,
Dean, College of Continuing Eduation

Hampton University, through its comprehensive activities, works assiduously to achieve its mission. Its reputation is renowned. Hampton University does indeed focus on students whose competencies are at a high level; however, through its many services, it supports the needs of the less generously endowed academically.

--Eleanor Lynch,
Former Director, The Honors College, and Associate Director, Center for Teaching Excellence

Hampton University, a progressive liberal arts college, has always been highly recognized for the programs in Nursing and Education. I have seen much growth in the fields of Pure and Applied Sciences as well as in the Humanities and Social Sciences. Programs in Computer Science and Mass Media have made excellent strides. Business (a very popular curricula) will become saturated over time, and I believe the Pure Sciences should be "pushed". . . . The Library has improved considerably and new technologies have been integrated. We still have much to add and accomplish. I believe that the new facility will provide more options and challenges. . . . We will need more professional help to respond to increased service needs, and to provide additional and more timely instructional programs. We are international information brokers who must interact, locate, and deliver (via the latest technology) those resources

demanded in the futuristic educational arena.
--Marilyn Loesch,
Librarian

The university is an exciting place with an outstanding President, who should be given the name of Builder of Hampton University. During his administration the school has made tremendous progress. According to future plans the Archives will have more space and hopefully an increase in personnel in order to give greater services to future generations.
--Fritz Malval,
Archivist

Hampton University is an outstanding university whose doors are always open to students who are ready to seek opportunities and challenges the university extends to them. Their stay at this university will prepare them to strive for excellence in their chosen field.
--Cora Reid,
Library Assistant

The preceding sampling of the insights of the faculty and staff reveals the futuristic dimension of the institution. Beginning with the 1991-92 academic year, a changed model began to evolve. As a result of retirement, the vice president for academic affairs left the administrative cabinet, and the vice president for administrative services became president of another university. During the second semester, the Vice President for Business Affairs and Treasurer retired from the position.

Aside from changes in personnel, it became apparent that Hampton University needed to review and document its recent past; thus the retired Vice President for Academic Affairs assumed the responsibility of focusing on developments during the 1978-91 era.

Long-range planning has been a critical part of the operations in every unit of the university during the Harvey era. However, as new challenges evolved, the president and board of trustees made a conscious decision to plan and prepare the university for leadership into the 21st Century. It became obvious that time would be taken to determine the future direction of Hampton University.

The 1992 Administrative Retreat was designed to develop plans for a year of strategic planning. To set the stage both President Harvey and Trustee Robert Binswanger both challenged and provided direction to the group.

Binswanger serves on the Academic Affairs Committee of the Board of Trustees and brings to the university a range of experiences in higher education among which are teaching at Harvard, Headmaster of the Boston Latin Academy and his current position as Professor at Dartmouth College. Steeped in knowledge and experience in higher education, Binswanger in his keynote address set the stage for the initiation of strategic planning at Hampton University.

Excerpt from Robert Binswanger's Address to Hampton University Administrators Administrative Retreat Hilton Head, South Carolina August 1992

What Is Strategic Planning?

You all have been planners since the day you entered this business of education. You did not have names, terms, models or courses, but you have been planners--good ones at that. As educators we have always been superb borrowers, doing more with less, and quick to pick up and adapt successful methods or practices in use elsewhere. As life became more complex, planning needed to adjust to the intricacies and interplay of complexity. Strategic planning was global, nuclear, and governmental. Then adopted by the multi-national businesses and mega corporations for planning finance, marketing and industry, then . .

. picked up by nations like Japan and Germany, Korea and Sweden, utilized by World Bank and various international bodies and now coming into higher education...It is vision management or for President Bush it is to define and implement his vision thing. It was C.P. Snow who said: "A sense of the future is behind all good policies. Unless we have it, we can give nothing either wise or decent to the world." The word "strategy" comes from the Greek "strategos", referring to a military general and combining "stratos" (the army) and "ago" (to lead). The association for the study of higher education in its 1984 Report #9 states the primary task are "to understand the environment, define organizational goals. Identify options, make and implement decisions and evaluate performance."

What It Is Not

It is not a departmental review where you look at everything with care and thoroughness in order to decide the need for more. It is not an accreditation [review] where you conduct a serious self-study, examine yourself, warts and all, and then clean up and hustle to present the most positive face to a peer committee that offers praise and platitudes fearful of candid criticism knowing that the tables can turn and you may be observing their institution so that the final report normally avoids the tough issues and steers away from an honest assessment. It is not the budget process, even if it is zero based, for we are all used to reviewing our own budgets in a hard-nosed approach in order to come up with the best strategies to get one more position, one piece of expensive equipment, additional computer use, and extra staff support--you know, in case of emergency. It is not developing a research proposal or a grant request, which by its nature tends to be insular and subject focused rather than an integral component part of the university--whether we are talking about course offerings, new academic initiatives, athletics, the museum, custodial staff, student center, library acquisitions, choir travel, scholarship aid, lab assistants, building renovations, graduate faculty--and the list is enormous if we focus on strategic planning. It is not long range planning which Peter Drucker says was to optimize for tomorrow the trends of today. No trends. No past modes or models. For Hampton this is new--planning to exploit the new and different opportunities for tomorrow. To be exploiters you must go on the attack. That was what Dr. Harvey meant last night in his reference to a searing self analysis. That is what he meant when he said the Trustees will reject pap and platitudes. The product is not the same old thing. I add two items to the fine charge delivered last evening to avoid any misconception. First, this will be the plan to chart Hampton's future but you are not planning for same actions to occur in the Year 2000. The actions will begin in 1993 and build and build so that by 2000 the plan is the institution. The plan is not immutable; it is not a process to be updated each August. It is instead a live flexible ongoing guide. In the 21st Century strategies may change but direction and mission remain clear. Secondly, the three categories--outstanding, good and phase-out need delineation. Outstanding in what we all strive to attain, every area, person or program cannot be excellent yet excellence is what is sought. As to good, there is nothing at Hampton if it is not good, one should not settle for less. That means the marching band, the campus shrubbery, faculty salaries, community service, counseling, classroom instruction, food service, the entrance sign--and if good is not the active goal, phase-out is merited. Hampton University cannot be all things to all people in 1992, 1996, 2000 or 2020!...

This process calls for everyone to get engaged and participate. The "it can't be done" group need to be striving for that good category or they should think of early retirement and relocation. It is not just faculty--the same groups are found in the ranks of administrators. You are the decision makers. Executives who execute decisions--carry them out. In this process you give up the power model--the distance--the participant observer role--the summary maker for the task is to open the door to all participants--faculty, staff, students, alumni, trustees. It is no easy assignment.

Challenge to the Administrators

Binswanger challenged the administrators to move with dispatch. He pointed out that:

This exercise is to be holistic. Nothing is left out, every item is reviewed, discussed and given a priority rating. The actions taken must be fundable. Some things will have to go. This planning process is linked directly to institutional character. Scan the horizon. Look at the total university. The process is not without pain. It will tax your energy and enthusiasm. Keep your eye on the prize. A premier higher education institution planned to operate in a first-class manner to aid and abet the lives of the young as they ready themselves for life in the 21st century.

This is your Hampton. What you do will make a difference. What you decide will impact student lives for years to come. Yours is a vital institution to America's future. This task will take from you. As you know, to give is to get. This will demand more than you imagined yesterday, but your efforts today will make for hundreds of better tomorrows.

REFERENCES

Bennis, Warren. Managing the dream: leadership in the 21st century. *Training: The Magazine of Human Resoures Development* (1990), 43-48.

Burling, Stacy. Hampton's best seller. *Virginia Magazine* (July 1983).

Cheney, Lynn. Fifty hours: A core curriculum for college students. *National Endowment for the Humanities*, Washington, DC (1989).

Dingle, Derek T. Hampton university's money magnet. *Black Enterprise* (Sept. 1985), 44.

Giancola, Patrice. HI selects president. The Newport News, VA *Times Herald* (March 1978).

Grossman, R.J. Wanted: New management style. *AGB Reports* (1990), 32,34-35.

Harwood, Markie. HI finishes fiscal year with surplus. The Newport News, VA *Times Herald* (Sept. 1982).

Harwood, Markie. HI Realizes 3rd straight budget surplus. The Newport News, VA *Times Herald* (Sept. 1981).

Lake, Marvin Leon. College defies odds in hard times. The Norfolk, VA. *Virginian Pilot* (June 1982), A1.

Lake, Marvin Leon. College picks president. The Norfolk,VA. *Virginian Pilot* (March 1978), A1, A4.

Lake, Marvin Leon. Hampton institute's president dedicated to excellence. The Norfolk, VA *Pilot* and *The Ledger-Star* (June 1978), B1, B4.

Number 12 for HI. Newport News, VA *Daily Press* (March 1978), 4.

Raspberry, William. Black college thrives in hard times. *The Washington Post* (April 1982), A31.

Timp, Phil. Hampton institute balances budget. Newport News, VA *Daily Press* (Sept. 1979), 12.

Timp, Phil. Harvey's dream coming true. The Newport News, VA *Daily Press* (Sept. 1979), 22.

Wash, Scott. Money, power and education. *Port Folio Magazine* (Feb. 1986).

INDEX

A Gathering of Old Men, 164
Academic Leadership Team
   (ALT), 47-51, 124
      Adjustments Teaching Load, 48
      Annual Increments For Scholarly Pursuits, 48
      Dean's Responsibility, 47
      Developing Networks, 47
      External & Internal Consultants, 48
      Recognition for Promotion & Tenure, 49
      Successful Fund Raising In An Era of Economic Decline, 50
      Technical Assistance, 47
      University Teamwork, 49
Academy Building, 3, 8
Adams, Ron, 152
Administrative Services Center, 94
Aetna Life & Casualty Foundation, 51
Airway Science Program, 145
Alewynse, John, iii, 128, 137, 138
Alumni Annual Fund, 57
American Archivist, 150
American Association of College Unions International, 111, 118
American Missionary Society, 2, 3
American Political Science Association, 161
American Revolution Bicentennial Administration, 8
American University, 161
Amoco Foundation, 57
Angelou, Maya, 118, 164
Applegate, James C., 128
Arab League, 161
Armstrong, General Samuel Chapman, ix, 2, 4, 6, 12, 15, 149, 151

Armstrong, Reverend Richard, 1
Armstrong Field, 6
Armstrong-Slater Hall, 108
Ashe, Arthur, 165
Askew, Robert, iii, 63
Assessment & Learning Support Center, 148, 153
Atkinson, Darryl, 115
AT & T, 56, 57, 58, 155
AT & T Bell Laboratory Library Network Summer Mentoring Program, 155
Bagley, Richard, 95
Baker, Dr. Gwendolyn, 123
Baraka, Amiri (LeRoi Jones), 164
Barbour, Lawrence P., 39
Baxter, Father, 17
Bean, Earl, iii, 139, 159, 171
Beaty, Dr. David, iii, 63
Belize, Central America, 68
Bennett, Dr. Lerone, 118
Bennis, Warren, 45
Berry, Dr. Joyce, 115
Biggers, John, 35, 91, 152, 163]
   House of the Turtle, 91
   Tree House, 91
Binswanger, Robert, 176
   Address to Hampton Administrative Retreat, 176-179
Black Enterprise, 32
Blalock, David, 26, 58
Bonner, Dr. Robert, iii, 60, 139, 171
Bowman, Dr. Ollie, 100, 107
Brazziel, Dr. William, 72
Brooks, Gwendolyn, 164
Brown, Dr. Carlton E., iii, 140, 157
Brown, Ronald, 165
Brown, Tony, 118
   Tony Brown's Journal, 98
Burling, Stacey, 29
Burroughs, Margaret, 164

Bush Foundation, The, 51, 52, 53, 58, 69, 72, 73, 74
Bush, President George, 32, 165, 168
C & P Telephone, 56
Cady, J. C., 3
Camp Young, 113
Campbell Soups, 28
Cappan, Lester J., 149
Carter, Dr. Alphonse, iii, 63, 64, 141
Carter, Roland, 14, 165
  "Hold Fast the Dream," 14
Catlett, Elizabeth, 152
Centennial Campus, 88
Center for Minority Special Education, 140
Center for Teaching Excellence, 68-74, 93, 143, 144, 174
Center Administration & General Services, 71, 72
  Course Planning & Development, 70-71
  Faculty Comments, 72-73
  Faculty Development & Evaluation, 69-70
  Instrumental Services Technical, 71
  New Faculty Evaluation Services, 73-74
  New Faculty Orientation & Development, 70, 74
Central America Peace Scholarship Program (CAPS), 68
Central Intercollegiate Athletic Association(CIAA), 16, 109, 110
Chapman, Ms. Barbara, 115
Children's Diagnostic Center., 64
Childress, Alice, 164
Christian, Dr. Mary T., 64, 141, 156
Civil Rights Act of 1964, x
Clark, Dr. Laron J., Jr., iii, 31, 50
Clark, Dr. Sulayman, 115
Cleckley, CAPT Julia, USA, 115
Cleveland, Charles Dexter, 4
  Cleveland Hall, 4
Clemson University, 184

College Choir, 14, 17
College of Continuing Education, 31, 102, 126, 143, 144, 152, 153, 172, 173, 174
College of William & Mary, viii, 145
Computer Science Program, 145
Conley, Dr. Harold W., iv, 142, 178
Contribution of the Negro to Democracy in America, 8
Conway, Ishmail, 115
Conaway, LeCount, iii
Cooper, Jorsene, iv, 159
Cornell University, 149
Cotter, Carrie, 115
Cotton, G. Robert, 58
Council for Financial Aid to Education, 32
Council of Academic Chairs (CAC), 124
Culbro Corporation, 56
Curtis, Ms. Woodrena, 116
Dana Foundation, Charles A., 57
Daniel, Dr. Elnora D., iv, 67, 143
David, Vivian, iv, 100, 158
Davidson Hall, 4
Davis Foundation, Arthur Vining, 54
Davis, Ossie, 165
Davis, LT Paul, USN, 116
Dawson, Dr. Martha E., 30, 47
Debs, Eugene, 20
Dee, Ruby, 165
Dellums, The Hon. Ronald V., 118
Delta Sigma Theta Sorority, 54
Department of Elementary Education, 146
Non-Graded Laboratory School, 146
Department of Energy, U.S., 76
Department of Finance, 186
Dett, Dr. Nathaniel, 6
Dickinson, Novelle, 116
Dorrance, John, 58
Dorrand, Jack, 28
Douglass, Frederick, 16
Drucker, Peter, 178
DuBois, W.E.B., 166

Duke University, 161
Duncan, John, 28, 58
Duncanson, CAPT Leo., USA, 116
Duplessis, Errol, 116
Early Childhood Laboratory School, 146, 147
Easter, Rufus, iv, 108, 171
Edgcombe, Frank B. iv, 172
Educational Testing Service (ETS), 124, 128
Ellinghaus, William (Bill), 28, 58
Emancipation Oak, 5, 8, 95
Emancipation Proclamation, 5
Eminent Presidential Scholars Program, 102, 144, 155
Endowed Scholarship, 156
Fears, Frederick, 116
Fears, Dr. Lois, 116
Federal Aviation Administration (FAA), 58
Ferris Foundation, Booth, 56, 57
Financial Corporation, 54
First Baptist Church in Hampton, 10
First National Conference on the Black Family, 17, 18
Fisk University, ix
Ford Foundation, 57, 151
Fort Monroe, 2
Fort Valley State University, 145
Foster, Dr. Gerald, 116
Founder's Day Ceremony, 38, 91
Fox, Edith Mead, 149
Freedman's Bureau, 2
Frissell, Hollis B., 2
Gaines, Ernest, 164
Garfield, President James, 16
Garrison, Professor Emeritus Hazel G., v, 132, 137, 143, 172
Gates, Paul, 149
Gardner, Dr. John N., 165
General Education Program, 129-137
General Electric Foundation, 56
General Mills Foundation, 56
General Motors Corporation, 54
Georgia State University, 72

Gossett, Lou, Jr., 164
Gouigis, Dr. Reginald, 116
Graduate College, 3, 126, 143, 151, 152, 153, 172
Gregg, James, 2
Guide to Hampton Institute Archives, 150
Hall, Reverend Leon B., 116
Hamilton, Ed, 163
Hampton Institute Historic Brochure, 1
Hampton Institute Mainstreaming Model (HIMM), 146
Hampton Institute Musical Arts Series, 16
Hampton, Lionel, 14
Hampton Script (The), 7, 8
Hampton University Archives, 153, 175
Hampton University Historic Brochure, 1
Hampton University Laboratory School, 64, 141, 146, 147
Hampton University Museum, 1, 16, 149, 150, 151, 152, 153
Hampton University Student Leadership Model, 118
Hardy, Dr. Vincent, 165
Harvard, 72, 145
Harvey, Dr. William R., vii, xi, 1, 3, 9-14, 50, 76, 78, 88, 91, 102, 110, 111, 119, 123, 129, 130, 131, 137, 138, 162, 170, 176, 178
  Inaugural Address, 15-23
  Impact as President, 24-46
  Significant External Appointments & Honors, 36-37
  Presidential Citation Award, 38-43
  William R. & Nora B. Harvey Library, xi, 35, 91, 159
  Charge, Graduating Class of '91, 166 - 167
Haysbert, JoAnn W., 126

Index

Hearst Foundation, William Randolph, 56
Heinemann, Edward A., 66
Henderson, James, 10, 162
Hill, Dr. Carl M., 3, 10
Hilliard, Professor Asa, 72
Hilo Training School, 2
Hines, Dr. Carolyn, 116
Historically Black College & University, vii
Holland, Jerome H., x, 3, 88
Holley, Ms. Anita, 116
Holmes Group, 157
Holmes, Dr. W. P., Jr., 91, 162
Holton, Governor Linwood, 28
Honors College, 104, 160, 174
Hoover, President Herbert, 6
Hopewell, Woodson, 116
Hopkins, Mark, 1
Housty, Dr. Enid P., iv, 66
Howard Hughes Medical Institute, 56
Howard University, 145, 161
Howe, Arthur, 2
Hudson, Dr. Roy D., 3, 10
Hughes, Langston, 23
Hunt, Richard M., 3, 92
Huntington, Mrs. Collis P., 4
  Huntington Memorial Building., 4
  Huntington Memorial Library, 91, 150, 159
Independence Foundation, 58
Indiana University, 141
International Business Machines (IBM), 52
International Understanding Program, 141
Jackson, Reverend Jesse, 165
Jeffries Trust Fund, 77
Johnson, Eugene W., 26, 122
Jones, Dr. Johnnie, 116
Jones, Dr. Reginald, iv, 66
Jones, Leonard, 116
Kearney, Dr. William, iv
Kellogg Foundation, W. K., 67
Kelsey Hall, 7
Kenan, Jr. Charitable Trust, 53
Kentucky State University, 10
Kiddie Kollege & Kiddie Kamp, 147-148
Knight, Alphonso, iv, 100, 173
Kollmann, Edward, 131
Kortunov, Andre, 163
Kresge Foundation, 53
Kuene, Daniel P., 66
Ladd Fund, Kate Macy, 58
Laflore, Ray L., v, 162
Lake, Marvin L., 11, 29
Lamb, Barbara M., v, 173
Langley Air Force Base, 6
Lawton, Dean Willie O., v, 144, 174
Lee, William E., 6
Lewis, Carvel, 168
  Responding to President Harvey's Challenge, 168-169
Lewis, Samella, 152
Lilly Endowment Inc. Foundation, 52, 142
Lincoln, Dr. C. Eric, 165
Little Scotland, 2
Livas Design Group, 91, 94
Locke, Dr. Mamie, 116
Loesch, Marilyn N., v, 175
Loyola University, 184
Lynch, Eleanor, v, 104, 132, 137, 160, 174
Mabuza, Hon. Lindewe, 163
MacLean, Malcolm, 3
Mahorn, Rick, 109
Maintenance Storage Facility, 24
Malval, Fritz J., v, 149, 150, 155, 175
Mansion House, 3, 8
Marine Science Building, 30, 34, 91
Marquand Estate, Fred. D., 3, 6
Marshall, General J. F. B., 5
Marshall-Palmer Hall, 4
Martin, Ann, 164
Massachusetts Institute of Technology, viii, 145
Mays, Dr. Nebraska, 123
McCloud, Dr. Patricia R., 118

McGhee, Dr. Nancy, xi
McGrew, Mrs. Hattie, 34, 92
  McGrew Towers, x, 30, 92
McKeithan, Ms. Sonya, 117
McLaughlin, Ms. Megan, 123
Mellon Foundation, Andrew W., 51, 54
Memorial Church/Chapel, 3, 8
Memorial Gardens, 95
Meyers, Dr. Samuel, 29
Mikalson, Jon D., 66
Mitchell, Eva C., 156
Modular Residence Halls, 30, 34
Moloto, Papie, 163
Mongella, Hon. Gertrude, 163
Monroe, Elbert B. & Mrs., 3
Moore, Ms. Frances, 117
Morehouse College, ix
Morgan Foundation, 52
Morrill Act, 6
Morris, Dr. Roberta, 117
Morrison, Toni, 164
Mott Foundation, Charles. S., 51, 52
Murray, Donald M., 128
Murray, Summer, 165
NASA, 22, 61, 62
National Association For Equal Opportunity In Higher Education (NAFEO), 29
National Association of Intercollegiate Athletics (NAIA), 109
National Bicentennial College, 8
National Center for Minority Special Education Research & Outreach, 66, 146
National Collegiate Athletic Association (NCAA), Division II, 109, 110
National Conference on Student Retention, 149
National Endowment of the Arts, 151
National Endowment for the Humanities, 66, 150
National Hampton Alumni Association, v, 100, 158
National Institutes of Health, 62
National Urban League's Junior Achievement Program, 63-64
National Science Foundation, 61, 62
Newport News *Daily Press*, 10, 26
Newport News *Times-Herald*, 27
Newsome, Ms. Veta, 116
Oberlin, viii
Ogden Hall, 4, 137, 138, 164
Ogden, Robert C., 4
Ohio State University, 141
Old Point Comfort, VA, 2
Old Testament, 20
Olin Engineering Building, xi, 34, 93
Olin Foundation, F.W., xi, 56, 58, 93
On-line Computer Library Center (OCLC), 138, 159
Organization of African Unity, 161
Packard Foundation, D. & L., 58
Painter, Carl, 109
Palmer Fund, 5
Palmer, General William Jackson, 5
  Palmer Hall, 5
Parker, Ernest, 117
Paterson, Katherine, 164
Peabody, George Foster, 5
Peabody Collection of African-American History & Affairs, 91
Peake, Mrs. Mary, 5
Perkins, Ms. Melba, 117
Petty, Dr. Linda, v, 69, 72, 74, 127, 144
Pew Memorial Trust, 51, 53
Phenix, George P., 2
  Phenix Hall, 159
  Phenix School, 7
Philip Morris Company, 54, 56, 57
Pierce, Sam, 28
Pinkett, Harold T., 150
Portfolio—the Magazine of Hampton Roads, 33
Pouissant, Dr. Alvin, 118

Prater, Dr. Oscar, v, 30, 102, 105, 106, 124, 145, 155
Presidential Citation to Community Leaders, 38
    Alexander, Mrs. Helen, 40
    Bagley, Hon. Richard M., 42
    Barbour, Lawrence P., 39
    Bolling, Mrs. Ellen L., 41
    Brauer, Mr. & Mrs. Harold A., Jr., 42
    Briggs, Joseph R., 41
    Chisman, Thomas P., 39
    Cotton, Dr. G. Robert, 39
    Cotton, James Alton, 40
    Cutler, Gordon B., 38
    Eason, Mrs. Midge Johnston, 43
    Ewell, Mrs. Alveta, 42
    Forst, Ms. Barbara, 42
    Gaines, Reverend Seymour, 40
    Gilliard, Joseph W., 42
    Harris, Edward F., 40
    Hassell, Richard, 43
    Hofheimer, Henry Clay, II, 41
    Jackson, Mrs. P. T., 41
    Kelly, Herbert V., Jr., 39
    Kilgore, Mrs. Ann, 38
    Kittrell, Dr. Flemmie P., 38
    Madden, Thaddeus Stevens, 40
    Magee, Mrs. Kathy S., 42
    Magee, Dr. William P., Jr., 42
    McGrew, Mrs. Hattie, 39
    Moore, Sylvius S., 41
    Nicholson, W. Edgar, 40
    Noel, Mrs. Rachel B., 41
    Overton, Hon. Nelson T., 42
    Parker, Henry "Hank" E., 38
    Parks, Mrs. Rosa, 39
    Rattley, Mrs. Jessie M., 39
    Reid, Dr. Milton A., 40
    Segaloff, Walter S., 42
    Sengstacke, John H., 38
    Tull, Knox W. 42
    Van Buren, Mrs. William R., 40
    Washington, Raymond G., 42
    White, Mrs. O'Marie N., 40
    Wright, Dr. Stephen J., 40
Princeton, viii
Project BEST, 68
Project HOPE, 105, 106
Project LEAP, 147
Purdue University, 141
Pyatt, Dr. Edward, v, 157
Quarter Century Club, 8
Queen Street Dormitory, 104
Raspberry, William, 28
Reagan, President Ronald, 27, 28, 32
Reid, Cora M., v, 156, 175
Robb, Sen./Gov. Chuck, 28, 32
Roberts, B.J., 117
Robinson, Dr. Dianne, v, 65
Robinson, Dr. Samuel, 123
Robinson, William H., 156
    Lecture Series, 157
Rockefeller Foundation, 56
Rockwell, Thomas, 164
Roosevelt, President Franklin D., 16
Rose, Don, 109
Rose, Ruth Starr, 14
Rouse, Parke, 1
SALT (Special Academic Leadrship Training), 122, 124
SAT, x, 32, 34, 102
Sanchez, Sonia, 164
Sarki, Ayuba v, 145, 159
Sceha, Dr. Boyd G., 123
School of Arts & Letters, 153
School of Business, iii, 63, 140, 141, 145, 153, 157, 158
School of Education, 64, 65, 141, 153, 156, 157
School of Library Arts & Education, iii, iv, 140, 153, 157
School of Nursing, iv, 67, 68, 142, 143, 153
School of Pure & Applied Science 60, 65, 93, 139, 153, 171
    Center for Marine & Enviromental Studies, 139

Center for Nuclear High Energy Physics, 139
Interdisciplinary Science Center, 65, 139
Mathematics Center for Computational Studies in Applied Mathematics, 139
Photonics Center ... Study of Optics & Lasers, 139
Schurz, Hon. Carl, 3
Schurz Hall, 3, 92
Science & Technology Building, 34, 69, 93
Screen, Dr. Robert M., v, 109
Shands, Ms. Cordelia, 117
"Shellbanks," 6
Shirley, George, 165
Simmons, Dr. Gertrude, 123
Sloan, Alfred P. Foundation, 52
Smith, David, 128
Snow, C. P., 177
Social Science Student Schools, 141
Southern Association of Colleges & Secondary Schools, 7, 8, 62
Southern Workman, 149
Spelman College, ix
Spencer, Thelma C., 128
Sprauve, Rodney, 117
St. Cyprian's Episcopal Church, 17, 156
Father Baxter, 17
St. Joe Minerals, 28
Stanford, viii
Staples, Robert, 99
Stone, Samuel & Mrs. Valerie, 4
Stone Memorial Building, 4
Strawn, Alexander, 107, 156
Summer Bridge Program, 105
Sun Company, 54
Sutton, LT Kenneth, USN, 117
Sweat, James, 109
Sweets, Dr. Loretta, 117
Symphonic Band & Terpsichorean Dance Troupe, 14, 17
Taft, President William Howard, 16

Taliaferro, Viola, Esq., 122
Taylor, Elizabeth, 28
Taylor, Hubert, 91
Taylor, Joyce, vi, 59
Taylor, O.G., 58
Teaching Learning Technology Center, 93, 143,159
Teagle Foundation, 57, 67
Thomas, Dr. Tobi, 165
Thompson, Marilyn, 165
Turner, Dr. Thomas Wyatt, 5
Turner Natural Science Building, 5
Tuskegee Institute, ix, 9, 10
Tuskegee News, 9
Twitchell Hall, 4
U.S. Coast Guard, 62
U.S. Department of the Army, 62
U.S. Department of the Army Civilian Personnel Managers, 63
U.S. Department of Education, 63, 149
U.S. Enviromental Protection Agency, 62
U.S. Naval Training School, 7
United Virginia Bank, 54
"University 101," 137-138
University of Delaware, 141
University of Michigan, 145
University of Notre Dame, viii
University of Richmond, 53
University of Rochester, 145
University of Toronto, 66
Univ. of Virginia, viii, 53, 66
University of Wisconsin-Madison, 66
Up From Slavery, 129
Upjohn, Robert, 58
Upjohn Pharmaceutical Co., 62
Upton, Robert, 58
Urasa, Dr. Isai T., vi, 62
Vann, MAJ Claude, III, vi
Venable, Demetrius, vi, 61
Victor, Dr. J., vi, 64, 66, 146
Virginia Foundation for the Arts, 151
Virginia Hall, 3, 4, 8, 92
Virginia Landmark Register, 8

Virginia Military Institute, 53
Virginia Polytechnic Institute, 53
Virginia Pilot and Ledger Star, 11, 29
Virginia United Methodist Assembly Retreat Center, 113
Virginia Wesleyan University, 113
Visions of Our Past, 1, 88
Volt, Stan, 9
Wade, Dr. Harold E., vi, 104, 105
Walters, Ms. Cheryle, 117
Wakefield 4-H Center, 113
Wallace, Peggy A., vi, 148
Walsh, Scott, 32, 33
Warfield, William, 165
Watson, Roger, 117
Washington, Booker T., ix, x, 16, 89, 95, 129, 163
Wharton School of Business, 145
Whipple Barn, 94
White, Charles, 8
Whitehead Foundation, L. Pate, 56
Whitmore, Yvonne, 72
Whittier, John G., 6
Whittier School, 6
Whittla, Dean, 72
Wigwam, 4, 8
Wilder, Governor L. Douglas, 32, 165
Wilder Hall, L. Douglas, xi, 92
Williams College, 1
Williams, Judge Joseph, 18
Williams, Ms. Julia G., vi, 117, 146
Wilson, Dr. Greer D., vi, 111, 118
Wilson, Dr. Wesley, 117
Winona Lodge, 4
Women's Educational Equity Act, 68
Woodrow Wilson Foundation, 161
Woods, Ms. Brenda, 117
Wyatt, Lucius, vi, 26, 30-31, 77, 78, 107, 123
Yale, viii
Zaki, Dr. Hoda M., vi, 160
Zeidler, Jeanne, 1, 151